LEADER
THE

LEADERSHIP IMAGES FROM THE NEW TESTAMENT
A Practical Guide

David W. Bennett

OM
publishing

Copyright © 1998 David W. Bennett

First published in 1998 by OM Publishing

04 03 02 01 00 99 98   7 6 5 4 3 2 1

OM Publishing is an imprint of Paternoster Publishing,
P.O. Box 300, Carlisle, Cumbria, CA3 0QS, U.K.
http://www.paternoster-publishing.com

British Library Cataloguing in Publication Data
A catalogue record for this book is available from the British Library.

ISBN 1-85078-309-8

Cover design by Mainstream, Lancaster.
Typeset by WestKey Ltd, Falmouth, Cornwall
Printed in Great Britain by Mackays of Chatham PLC, Kent

Contents

Why are Metaphors so Important for Christian Leaders?

During his three years of public ministry, Jesus focused much of his time and attention on the development of the twelve people who would become the leadership core of the earliest Christian community. Yet the words 'leader' and 'leadership' do not appear in the gospels. In fact, Jesus says surprisingly little to his disciples about their future role as leaders.

Why is this? Could it be that leadership has more to do with learning to *follow* than with learning to command, supervise, or manage? Could it be that effective leadership depends more on right attitudes than on the mastery of certain skills? Could it be that it is more important for the leader to understand what he or she has in common with other followers of the Lord than to focus on what sets the leader apart from the rest?

Leadership has been defined as a process of influence. To understand how Jesus prepared the disciples to be leaders, we can begin by studying what he said about how they would influence others. Even though we do not find detailed job descriptions for the disciples in Scripture, we can find passages that detail the impact that Jesus expected them to have on the lives of others. Many of these insights are embedded in the images which Jesus used to describe his followers. Terms like 'witness', 'servant', 'salt', and 'harvester' are full of implications for the role of the spiritual leader.

A metaphor, or image, helps us to understand a concept in terms of something with which we are already familiar. With a creative leap of imagination, we are able to perceive a point of similarity, or to open up a new avenue of insight. Imagery becomes especially important when we try to understand a God whom we cannot see and realities that transcend space and time. We need images to help us to comprehend not only the spiritual community of which we are a part, but also the place of leadership in that community. A study of images of leadership must include images of the church in which these leaders function.

There is no single 'master image' which fully embraces the totality of church life and leadership. Each picture allows us to view the whole from a somewhat different perspective. It is only as we combine and compare the different perspectives that we will begin to develop an understanding of the totality that they describe. There are many debates in the church today about the most appropriate images to capture the imaginations of present-day Christians and to direct and inspire the work of church leaders. But the place to begin is with a thorough understanding of the metaphors that Jesus introduced to his disciples.

2

Why Did Jesus and the Apostles Select the Metaphors They Did?

Jesus and his apostles had many choices in what they said and in the roles with which they decided to identify. We can learn much from the words they chose to use as well as those they avoided. Jesus chose terms suited to his listeners, and whose associations reinforced the lessons he was trying to teach. He used images that were appropriate to the culture, appropriate to the disciples' stage in the process of leadership development, and appropriate to the particular circumstances in which he taught them.

Jesus drew his illustrations, or metaphors, from the common materials of life that would have been familiar to his hearers. He spoke of relationships in the family, of children with their father, and brothers with sisters. He described ordinary scenes from the household – the preparation of meals, work in the fields.

Some of his illustrations came from everyday work – shepherds and fishermen, land owners and managers, court officers and personal assistants. Other metaphors were drawn from common social relationships and community celebrations – friends and associates, members of the wedding party and guests at a banquet. Everyday objects and sights were used to teach lessons in discipleship – salt, lamps, vines, flocks of sheep and goats, ripe fields of wheat, beaten down pathways, thorns and rocks. Some of Jesus' illustrations echoed the images used by prophets of Israel from centuries before – the chosen people, the servant, the vine, the brother, the friend of God, the messenger.

Jesus was speaking mainly to the common people, whose lives were intertwined with their fields and their flocks, or their boats and their nets. Therefore most of his illustrations were drawn from these spheres. His metaphors needed no explanations. They carried familiar associations of smell and feel and sound. They evoked feelings and memories. People had watched virgins with their lamps at weddings and had listened to the testimony of witnesses before a judge. They used salt to preserve their food and had heard children calling to one another in the market-place.

The strength of a metaphor is that it awakens associations, stirs emotions, and embodies values. It focuses our attention, highlighting certain details, and encourages creative new insights. But the power of a metaphor depends largely on the familiarity of the image that serves as the basis for the comparison. An illustration that must first be explained in order to be appreciated loses much of its impact. Jesus chose metaphors that were close to his listeners.

Jesus did not introduce lots of metaphors at once in his encounters with his disciples. Certain patterns can be discerned in the arrangement of, and emphasis on, certain illustrations at different points in the disciples' pilgrimage.

To begin with, all four gospel writers cite metaphors that focus on the task as the earliest ones used by Jesus. Matthew and Mark record the statement, 'Follow me, and

I will make you fishers of men' (Mt. 4:19; Mk. 1:17). In the parallel account in Luke, Jesus says to Peter the fisherman, 'From now on you will catch men' (Lk. 5:10). John does not record the call of the fishermen but does report another incident from early in Jesus' ministry – the encounter by the well in Samaria. There Jesus invites the disciples to join him in the work of spiritual harvest (Jn. 4:35–38). Thus Jesus' initial call to the disciples was to join him in a task – proclaiming the good news of the kingdom of God, inviting lost men and women to repent and believe and to join the community of the Messiah.

Jesus' last words to the disciples contained a similar emphasis on the task. He reminded them that they were to be his 'witnesses', and he commissioned them to go and 'make disciples' of all the nations. But in between the initial call and the final commission, Jesus consistently emphasized images that spoke of the close relationships into which his followers were being called.

The focus on relationships began very early in Jesus' instructions to his disciples. Numerous times in the Sermon on the Mount (Matthew 5–7) Jesus spoke of the disciples as children of the heavenly Father and as brothers of one another. In Mark 2 Jesus compared his disciples to friends of the bridegroom who were so caught up in the joy of the celebration that they could not think of sombre activities like fasting. The next chapter records the occasion on which Jesus said that those who did the will of God were his brother and sister and mother (Mk. 3:31–35).

The themes of brotherhood and a father/child relationship to God remain prominent throughout Jesus' ministry to his disciples. But the most intimate description of Jesus' love for the disciples, and theirs for him, does not come until the night of the Last Supper, in John 15. There Jesus

says, 'I no longer call you servants. . . . Instead, I have called
you friends' (Jn. 15:15). The 'task' word, 'servant', although
an accurate description of the relationship in many respects,
is no longer adequate; it cannot express the intimate love,
or the free communication, that exists between Jesus and
his followers. The word 'friend' must be summoned into
service. Jesus could not have made such a statement early
in his ministry, before the bonds of deeper trust and
commitment had been forged with the disciples through
months of travel and ministry together. Some metaphors
were appropriate from the very outset; others needed more
time to become relevant.

The whole cluster of 'servant' images becomes much
more prominent in Jesus' teaching toward the end of his
ministry, as he and the disciples make their way to Jerusalem
for the last time. The disciples are finally understanding that
Jesus is the Messiah, the Son of God. Following Peter's clear
profession of faith at Caesarea Philippi, Jesus begins to speak
more frequently of his impending sufferings. But the disciples are filled with visions of the coming glories of the
kingdom; they are thrilled with the prospect of sitting on
their thrones judging the twelve tribes of Israel. Soon the
seeds of ambition begin to erupt in open competition and
arguments. So Jesus begins to speak more often of the role
of the servant, who places himself humbly at the disposal
of the other, and who willingly follows his master along
the path of suffering. Thus almost all of the servant teachings of Jesus are found in the later chapters of the gospels,
in Matthew 18–25, Mark 9–13, Luke 12–22, and John
12–15. The longer a person has been involved in the
process of leadership development, the more likely it is that
he may start to struggle with ambitious pride and may need
to be reminded that his purpose is to serve, not to rule.

It is also significant that Jesus did not refer to any of the disciples as 'shepherd' until after the resurrection, when he spoke to Peter in John 21. Until that time, the emphasis is on their role as 'sheep'. The crucial lesson for each disciple to learn early was how to be a follower. Only after he had learned to follow well could he be trusted to lead.

Jesus chose his illustrations wisely in view of the particular circumstances of the people he was addressing. For example, when he extended the initial call to fishermen by the lake shore, he promised to make them 'fishers of men'. But as far as the gospel writers record, he did not use this metaphor again, because the others he called were from different vocations.

When speaking of the interpersonal tensions that were bound to arise in a closely knit community, Jesus reminded the disciples that they were brothers. He knew that they would be tempted, when injured, to put distance between themselves; but he insisted that they recognize the bonds that joined them as members of the same spiritual family.

When arguments arose among the twelve concerning who was to be the greatest, Jesus responded by setting a child in the midst of them as an illustration, or by describing the characteristics of a servant. When his followers began to assume that the kingdom was going to be established in the very near future, Jesus told parables that pictured servants whose masters went away for long periods of time, servants who were responsible to make wise investments in the meantime.

Jesus drew his illustrations from numerous objects, activities, and roles of everyday life. Yet there are some significant omissions. There are a number of words that Jesus does *not* use for his followers, even though these social roles would have been very familiar to Jesus' listeners.

In the first place, Jesus does not use any of the numerous words compounded from the Greek root *arch-*, which have to do with rule and which carry a strong tone of authority. Although Jesus tells numerous stories involving masters and servants, and often uses the word 'master' (*kyrios*), he never compares his disciples to the master – only to the servants. Even the illustrations of those who have responsibility over others feature those who are themselves servants – the steward (*oikonomos*) who manages his master's household and possessions, or the shepherd (*poimen*) who tends the flock of another.

Jesus describes his followers as a family, but he never refers to any of the disciples as a 'father'. On the contrary, in Matthew 23:9 he warns, 'Do not call anyone on earth "father", for you have one Father, and he is in heaven.' Even in the passages where he speaks so clearly of his followers as a spiritual family, he refers to 'brother and sister and mother', but not to 'father' (Mt. 12:50; Mk. 3:35; Lk. 8:21). We have already noted Jesus' reserve in speaking of the disciples as shepherds until late in his ministry with them – and even then, the focus is on the tender care of the shepherd for the sheep, not on the authority with which he leads them.

Yet the references to *following* are very numerous – the disciple (*mathetes*) following the teacher, the servant the master, the sheep the shepherd. Jesus places far more emphasis in the development of his disciples on their following than on their leading. He avoids altogether the terms that evoke images of strong authority, or that encourage comparison with political rulers. He uses many more images that encourage the disciples to think of themselves as 'among' or 'under' than 'over' others.

Another set of images notable by their absence are those drawn from the temple and its worship. Although the apostles Paul, Peter, and John each take up the metaphor of 'priest' in the description of the believer, Jesus never does. Perhaps because of the corruption of so much of the temple worship in Jesus' day, as well as the opposition from so many of the priests, and the involvement of the chief priests in political manoeuvres with the Roman government, Jesus chose not to draw illustrations from this sphere. With his emphasis on the disciples as brothers to one another, Jesus may also have wanted to avoid any hints of elitism implied in the use of priestly language.

3

What Themes Run Through the Biblical Metaphors?

Seven fundamental themes emerge repeatedly in the images used by Jesus to describe his disciples. These themes form the basis of the style of life for which Jesus was preparing his followers. These patterns would shape the early Christian community and would become the standards for its leaders. As we explore the ways in which the metaphors introduced by Jesus are taken up by the writers of the early church, we discover these same seven themes continuing to recur.

Although the New Testament writings show considerable diversity in style, vocabulary, and imagery, a deep underlying unity becomes evident when we look at the basic ideas about discipleship and leadership that are expressed. We find that we are not listening to new and original melodies, but to variations on a theme. We do not uncover totally new patterns of thought and life, but new perspectives and further insights into teaching already given by Jesus to his followers.

Theme #1 (Function) – *The disciple is called to participation in a community as well as to a task*

A number of metaphors highlight the bond of commitment and love that tie the followers of Jesus to one another and to their Lord, while others emphasize the mission for which the disciples have been enlisted. The words that speak of the relationship between Jesus and his followers include child (*hyios, teknion, teknos, nepios, paidion*), friend (especially *philos*), disciple (*mathetes*), and sheep (*probaton*); the words brother (*adelphos*) and sister (*adelphe*) point to the connection between the followers. On the other hand, the whole cluster of servant words (including *doulos* and *diakonos*), as well as several other images like apostle (*apostolos*), fisherman (*halieus*), shepherd (*poimen*), salt (*halas*), and light (*phos*), focus on the disciple's life of active service and influence in the world, carrying out the task of ministry in Jesus' name.

We cannot read the New Testament letters and the book of Acts without being impressed by the depth of loving commitment that tied the early Christian communities together. The frequent affectionate references to one another as brother and sister, and the tender parental concern shown by the apostles toward the congregations they established and nurtured, testify to the warmth and strength of the bonds of this new spiritual family. The many appearances of the word for household (*oikos*) and related terms, descriptions of believers as a chosen people, and the frequent use of images such as the building and the body express the essential unity of the church.

During the Last Supper, Jesus spoke at length about the love for one another that would be the hallmark of his true followers. In the remainder of the New Testament we see much more about the ways in which that love was expressed. In the gospels, the competition between the disciples is often more evident than their teamwork; but in the early church we observe numerous 'fellow' (*sun*) compounds – fellow-worker, fellow-citizen, fellow-athlete, fellow-soldier, yokefellow, fellow-elder, fellow-member, fellow-heir, fellow-imitator – all expressing a co-operative and sympathetic spirit of oneness. Other images express the bonds that tie believers together as imitators of one another, as followers of the same Way, as sheep led by the same shepherds, as branches grafted into the same tree, and as a body that suffers and rejoices with each of its members. Although the differences between believers are acknowledged, images like that of the body show that there is unity amidst the diversity of gifts.

The community unites, but it also separates. The heavenly citizenship that brings Jews and Gentiles together simultaneously makes them aliens and strangers to their own society. The call to be saints involves separation from the world. As light Christians are responsible to expose and rebuke the darkness.

The metaphors of the New Testament letters often highlight the privileges that accompany membership in the community – such as the bride's experience of her husband's loving nurture, the slave set free, the son adopted into the family, the temple as the dwelling of God's Spirit, and the church as God's chosen people and treasured possession. The disciples can rejoice not only in all the new dimensions of relationship to one another, but also in the intimacy of fellowship with the Lord who has called them his friends.

Yet, the emphasis on community does not overshadow the importance of the task given to followers of Jesus Christ. The metaphors drawn from priesthood and temple, including words for 'serve' like *latreuo* and *leitourgeo*, point to the duties of worship, praise, and thanksgiving, as well as to the consecration of the entire life as a type of spiritual sacrifice. The church is called to serve and to build up one another through the functioning of the spiritual gifts in the body, through acts of imitating and modelling, and through nurturing younger believers as parents nurture children.

The primary focus of the church's service in the world is presented as the proclamation of the good news of Jesus Christ, expressed through the use of terms like apostle, evangelist, herald, and ambassador. Broader dimensions of service and good works are implied in images like light, stars, and fragrance. This engagement with the world involves conflict. The images of striving as an athlete in competition, and fighting as a soldier with the forces of darkness, appear frequently.

In addition to the tasks to which every follower of Jesus is called, several images accent the specific and different tasks for which various ones are responsible as stewards of different parts of the household, or as different members of the body. In particular, new terms are introduced in the rest of the New Testament that apply specifically to leaders within the fellowship – words such as overseer (*episkopos*), administration (*kybernesis*), elder (*presbyteros*), and leader (*prohistemi*), in addition to the further development of terms like shepherd (*poimen*), apostle (*apostolos*), and leader (*hegemonos*) that were used by Jesus. In the gospels, the main emphasis is on the responsibility of the disciple as servant to follow; but the remainder of the New Testament reveals more of the dimensions of responsibility and oversight to which various servants are assigned.

So then, both dimensions of community and task remain equally prominent throughout the New Testament; but it is very easy for the spiritual leader to lose this balance

between task and relationship. Some become so intent on
nurturing the community of faith as a loving family that
they become ingrown, neglecting the tasks of evangelism
and service to the world. Others become so goal-oriented
and determined to mobilize every believer for action that
they do not pay sufficient attention to the needs of the
people for personal nurture, encouragement, and reconciliation. Jesus' disciples are to remember that they are *both*
brothers/sisters *and* servants.

Theme #2 (Authority) – *The disciple is under authority*

Over half of the metaphors chosen by Jesus describe someone who is under the authority of another. Often the word
selected is one member of a familiar role pair, such as child
(of a father, *pater*), servant (of a master, *kyrios*), or disciple
(of a teacher, *didaskalos*). Other images of those under
authority include the shepherd (*poimen*) who tends a flock
that belongs to another, the worker (*ergates*) hired by the
landowner (*oikodespotes*), the apostle (*apostolos*) commissioned by his superior, and the sheep (*probaton*) obeying the
voice of the shepherd.

It is interesting to note that even though the disciples
are being prepared for spiritual leadership in the church,
Jesus places far more emphasis on their responsibility to
God's authority, than on the authority which they themselves will exercise. There is far more instruction about the
role of following than about the role of leading.

The image of the servant under authority remains a
central theme in the New Testament letters. The apostles
describe themselves as servants of Christ. Even the freedom

of the Christian is seen as freedom to serve, not as absolute autonomy. Terms that imply one who is under authority include frequently used words like sheep, soldier, steward, and apostle, as well as terms like ambassador, pilot, herald, and vessel. Christ is the head of the body, and the cornerstone of the building. He is the chief shepherd of the flock.

A new dimension of living under authority that emerges in the early church stems from the authority exercised within the community by its human leaders. Believers are called to obey their leaders, to respect them, and to submit to them. To describe elders as shepherds and overseers is to imply that the congregation must follow their direction. The call to imitate Christian leaders is a call to accept their authority.

To be a disciple is also to live under the authority of the Word of God. The image of the athlete is associated with the need for strict training and discipline, another expression of life under authority.

Theme #3 (Responsibility) – *The disciple exercises authority*

The emphasis of Jesus' instruction is on obedience to authority rather than on the exercise of authority; nevertheless Jesus does employ images that describe the follower as one who is given responsibility for others. On two occasions, Jesus promises the twelve that in his coming kingdom they will sit on thrones judging the twelve tribes of Israel (Mt. 19:28; Lk. 22:30); this is a strong and unmistakable image of authority.

In his parable about the manager (*oikonomos*) in Luke 12, Jesus pictures the disciple as one who is placed in charge of other people as well as possessions. Similarly, in the parable of the ten minas (Lk. 19:12–27), the faithful servants are rewarded by being given responsibility over entire cities. Jesus' instructions to Peter in John 21 about performing the work of a shepherd also imply a role of leading and guiding within the Christian community. Jesus' words to the apostles contain clear statements concerning the authority which they would exercise over demons. As ones sent by God, the apostles proclaim the message about the coming kingdom with the very authority of God; in fact, says Jesus, the one who receives them is receiving the One who sent them.

Therefore, there is no contradiction in Jesus' mind between being under authority and being responsible to exercise authority. Frequently in the gospel of John, Jesus speaks of his own obedience as the Son to the Father, yet in John 13 he affirms that the disciples are correct to call him their master and teacher.

After Jesus' ascension to heaven, the role of leadership in the Christian community undergoes considerable development. Prophets and apostles provide overall direction for the church based on the authoritative proclamation of the Word of God. Various leadership gifts then begin to function. Soon elders and deacons are appointed to oversee the affairs of local congregations. Several of the terms used specifically imply the provision of direction and the exercise of authority – especially apostle (*apostolos*), overseer (*episkopos*), leader (*hegemonos* and *prohistemi*), administrator (*kybernesis*), manager (*oikonomos*), shepherd (*poimen*), and elder (*presbyteros*).

In addition to these specific roles of authority, believers in general are appointed to positions of responsibility by the risen Lord. All are instructed to exercise their spiritual gifts as stewards, or managers (*oikonomoi*), of the many-faceted grace of God. As a kingdom of priests, all are promised a share in Christ's rule in the coming kingdom. All are invited to represent the King of Kings as his ambassadors, proclaiming the message of reconciliation.

Theme #4 (Derivation) – *The disciple is one who has responded to the call of Jesus*

The statement of this theme has two aspects. In the first place, it emphasizes that God is the initiator; everything comes from him and starts with him. On the other hand, to be a disciple is to respond willingly to the call, not to be conscripted as an unwilling recruit.

No matter how much authority disciples may exercise, their roles and responsibilities are always derived from their prior call. The disciple is fundamentally a responder, not an initiator. As Jesus reminds the disciples in John 15:16, 'You did not choose me, but I chose you.' The disciple is a branch of the vine, not the vine itself; apart from the vine the branch can produce nothing. The disciple has no philosophy of his own to expound; he is only an 'apostle' (*apostolos*), a messenger commissioned by another. He is a servant assigned to a master, a child born to a father, a guest invited to a wedding, soil receiving the implanted seed. Yes, there are images of growth and influence – but the source of life lies elsewhere, not in the disciple himself.

This theme is closely related to the theme of authority. But it goes even deeper. Jesus reminds the disciple through these images that *everything* comes from God. As Jesus expresses it in John 15:5, 'Apart from me you can do nothing.' To use a different metaphor, the spiritual leader is not a creative musician, composing his own tunes; rather he is an arranger of the song sung by the Master. Nor is the leader an inventor and entrepreneur, dreaming up a product and then marketing it; rather he is the distributor for a precious commodity supplied to him. The disciple is not autonomous; he lives in relationship to a fixed reference point – the life, the word, and the example of his Master.

Just as Jesus did, the New Testament writers place great emphasis on the gracious call of God. The very word church (*ekklesia*) pictures an assembly that has gathered in response to a call. Paul describes himself as called to be an apostle, and appointed to be a herald; he says that by God's grace he has been allowed to lay the foundation upon which others are building. The grace, mercy, and love of God are the foundations for our adoption as God's children and his choosing us as a holy nation.

The complete dependence of the church on Christ is expressed in the pictures of Christ as head of the body and cornerstone of the building. The sheep cannot survive apart from the Great Shepherd. Although one plants and another waters, it is God who causes the growth. Every enablement for ministry is a spiritual gift distributed according to God's design. The evangelist, the prophet, and the herald pass on messages, not of their own invention but given to them by God. Each believer is a 'new creature', endowed with life that only God can create. Even our very physical existence is like a mist, here only for as long as God's grace allows.

Yet the New Testament images do not express God's initiating role alone. They also indicate the importance of willing human response. The follower of Jesus is a disciple, an imitator, a follower of the Way, a believer.

Theme #5 (Status) – *Disciples are on the same level in relationship to God, even though they may have different areas and amounts of responsibility*

In Matthew 23 Jesus reminded the disciples in very strong terms that they were all brothers, all children of one father, all students at the feet of the same teacher. Among the followers of Jesus there were to be none of the status-seeking games and political manoeuvres that characterized the life of the Pharisees. On other occasions as well, Jesus contrasted the life of servanthood with the grasping for power and the abuse of authority that was so typical of pagan rulers. The disciples were not to strive for the right to be 'over', but rather were to focus on their role 'among', as brothers, and on occasion to place themselves 'under', as servants.

On the other hand, Jesus was not establishing a kind of radical egalitarianism where any sort of internal authority structure in the community was seen as a denial of brotherhood, or where any difference in level of responsibility was regarded as an attack on the principle of spiritual equality. Rather his illustrations, such as the parable of the minas and the talents, described believers who were given differing degrees of responsibility. And as has been noted already, Jesus' references to the apostle, the shepherd, and the manager are images that imply the existence of authority roles within the community.

Jesus' focus is not on particular structures of leadership in the community, but rather on the attitudes that should characterize the leaders. He tells his disciples that even the teachers of the law and the Pharisees should be obeyed in their role as teachers of the Mosaic law (Mt. 23:2), but that their hypocritical *practices* must be rejected. Jesus himself never surrendered his authority role within the twelve, yet he called the disciples his brothers and his friends.

Although different levels of responsibility and authority become increasingly evident as the early church develops and becomes more organized, most of the New Testament imagery emphasizes what believers have in common, rather than the ways in which they are different.

On the one hand, there are terms that indicate that no one is higher than anyone else. The ministry of all, including apostles, is called simply service as a waiter (*diakonia*). Even the greatest leader is no more than a servant of the Master. All are children of God, and brothers and sisters to one another. Paul describes himself as a common clay pot holding the priceless treasure of the gospel. Both the one who plants and the one who waters the field are merely doing the task assigned to them.

On the other hand, there are numerous terms indicating the high status that all believers now enjoy because of their union with Christ. Privileges that other societies confer on only a few are now the possession of even the humblest Christian. Each one is a royal priest. Each shares in the rule of Christ's kingdom. Each has been adopted as a child of God. Each one's body is a temple of the Holy Spirit. Each is a full citizen in the new Jerusalem. Each is called saint, chosen, beloved, freedman, heir, and treasure.

Yet functional differences remain. Wives are still to be subject to their husbands, children are to obey parents, slaves are to serve their masters cheerfully. Members of the congregation are told to obey and to submit to their leaders, and to keep on paying taxes and giving respect to government authorities. But the one with authority is to remember that he or she is not better than the others, and the one under authority is to remember the dignity and freedom of his or her calling. Whatever may be their differences in social standing in the eyes of society, or their various responsibilities in the church, they are first and foremost partners, fellow-workers, fellow-heirs, children of the same Father.

Theme #6 (Identification) – *To be a disciple is to identify with Jesus, both in his pattern of life and in his suffering*

As Jesus says in Luke 6:40, 'Everyone who is fully trained will be like his teacher.' To be a disciple, Jesus emphasizes, is not merely to comprehend a body of truth, or even to perform an assigned task, but rather to adopt a pattern of life. Jesus defines 'disciple' in terms of unqualified commitment and firm adherence to Jesus' words and patterns of love. He uses the image of the child to emphasize that the child should resemble the heavenly Father. The disciple is described as salt and light. Thus true disciples are not to be identified simply on the basis of their knowledge, or their accomplishments, but on the basis of their character, their attitudes, their commitments – in short, their *likeness* to Christ.

One of the sternest tests of identification with Jesus is the willingness to participate in his sufferings. The images of the servant (*doulos* and especially *diakonos*) as well as the witness (*martys*) are closely associated with the experience of hardship and persecution. In John 12 Jesus also uses the image of the kernel of wheat which must fall into the ground and die in order to be fruitful.

Spiritual leadership is not a position of privilege which exempts one from suffering. Rather the leader, like Jesus, must be willing to be the first to set the example of laying his life down and of obeying at the cost of death. The leader must not be like the hired hand who runs away and deserts the sheep when he sees the wolf coming. Rather, the leader must be prepared to share in his Master's suffering. As Jesus said, 'Whoever serves me must follow me; and where I am, my servant also will be' (Jn. 12:26).

To follow Jesus is not simply to accept a body of beliefs but to adopt a pattern of life. To be Jesus' disciple is to become like him. This emphasis on life transformation and training through personal identification is continued in the New Testament through the use of terms like imitator, disciple, model, and follower of the Way.

The distinctive identification of the believer with the life of Jesus Christ is implied in the application of the nickname 'Christian', and in the call to behave like an alien and a temporary resident. The child of God is expected to be holy as is the heavenly Father. The fragrance of the believer's life is supposed to make people aware of Jesus.

Identification with Jesus means not only imitation of his character but also participation in his mission, even to the point of suffering and death. Many of the New Testament images are associated closely with the suffering that the believer will experience for Christ's sake. The apostles lead the way into the arena of death, and they are seen by many as the scum and refuse of the earth. The saints in the book of Revelation endure through tribulation. The athlete must run the race with endurance and wrestle with the forces of darkness. The witness often becomes the martyr. The Christian as soldier contends with deadly opposition and can survive only as protected by God's armour. To be an alien is to be excluded and sometimes persecuted for one's differences. To serve is to suffer.

The leader is not exempt in any way from these hardships and sacrifices. Rather the leader is to be the model of pouring out one's life as a sacrificial offering.

Theme #7 (Accountability) – *The disciple will be evaluated by the Lord, in terms of his character as well as his service*

Many of Jesus' illustrations draw a contrast between effectiveness and ineffectiveness in service, between those who fulfill their intended purpose and those who do not. The good salt is contrasted with the salt that has lost its savour. The lamp is intended to be placed on the lamp stand, not to be hidden under a bowl. Some branches remain in the vine and become fruitful; others do not, so are cut off. The good soil produces crops of thirty, sixty, or one-hundred times what was planted; but neither the pathway, the rocky soil, nor the thorny soil yield anything of value.

The good shepherd, who cares for the sheep, is contrasted with the hired hand who has no personal commitment to their welfare. Some virgins provide extra oil for their lamps; others fail to do so. The unprofitable servant does only his duty; the irresponsible manager fails to provide for the other household servants.

Repeatedly, Jesus' parables make reference to rewards – the master's words of 'Well done', the assignment of responsibility over cities, the promise of ruling on thrones. But equally often there are references to disciplines and punishments – a guest without a wedding garment thrown outside into the darkness, an unfruitful branch cut off, a lazy and unproductive servant stripped of his responsibility.

Through images like these Jesus teaches that discipleship is serious business. It is more than participation in the life of a warm and loving family. The disciple is held responsible for growth in character development and for productive investment of resources and opportunities. A time of judgement is coming, when the disciple's life and work will be evaluated; and there will be losses as well as rewards. The spiritual leader is not exempt from this evaluation, any more than any other disciple.

Just as Jesus contrasted those who were faithful and effective servants with those who were not, so the New Testament writers speak of vessels of honour and dishonour, fields that produce a crop and others that drink the same rain but yield only thistles, those who have matured and those who remain as infants, those who have become teachers and those who still must be taught. The athletic images illustrate again and again that there is a prize to be won, a crown to be awarded, but that not everyone will even finish the race, let alone be honoured as a victor.

Fellow-believers may presume to evaluate one another's performance. But several images suggest caution. The believer is a servant who stands or falls to his own master (Rom. 14:4). Paul claims that his faithfulness in stewardship is known only to the Lord, who will make the true assessment at the last judgement (1 Cor. 4:1–5). He defends himself before his critics by saying that the churches he has planted stand as his crown, his seal, his letter of recommendation. The evaluation for which the believer must prepare is the one that will take place at the judgement seat of Christ (2 Cor. 5:10).

4

What Conclusions Can we Draw for Christian Ministry Today?

Leadership is a process of influence. Even though Jesus did not use the words 'leader' or 'leadership', he called his disciples into a development process, through which he prepared them for leadership in the Christian community after his ascension.

Yet Jesus' primary focus in teaching the disciples was not to help them to master the skills often associated with leadership – setting goals, formulating strategies, organizing personnel and resources, exercising authority and discipline. He gave almost no direction about how the early Christian community should be organized, how authority should be delegated, how decisions should be made, how visions should be translated into action, or how others should be mobilized or equipped for the task.

Instead, Jesus showed his disciples how to follow, how to obey, how to respond to the authority and call of God. He knew that the effective leader must first learn how to be a faithful follower. Jesus also knew how destructive the attitudes of pride and ambition could be within the community of disciples. Therefore, he taught them attitudes of humility and self-sacrifice, using the image of the servant, and reminded them of their equal standing before God as brothers. Jesus wanted his disciples to think of themselves as 'among' one another, as brothers, and 'under' one another, as servants, more than 'over' one another, as those in authority.

Jesus was also concerned to help the disciples realize that they were being called to significant relationships as well as to important tasks. They were not just workers; they were also friends. They were not only fishers of men, but also guests at a wedding. Celebration and joy and love were to be as much a part of their vocabulary as responsibility and accountability and diligence. They would be evaluated by their love for one another, and by their personal commitment to Jesus, as well as by their faithfulness in completing their assigned tasks and investing their divinely-given resources.

Variations on a Theme

To impart such lessons as these, Jesus used many images. The primary images used by Jesus can be grouped into two categories – those that describe the followers as members of a spiritual family (brother, child), and those that picture them as servants (of the Lord and of one another). The first group focuses on relationships. The second group focuses on the task.

These same two clusters of images remain in the foreground throughout the rest of the New Testament writings. Some new terms are added, but the essential emphasis remains the same – the Christian has been incorporated into a loving, interdependent family, and has been commissioned to serve the Lord as part of the mandate to make disciples of all the nations.

What it means to be a follower of Jesus remains consistent throughout the New Testament. The seven fundamental themes are revealed in the teaching of the epistles as fully as in Jesus' instructions to his disciples. In the epistles implications are spelled out in more detail, and new images are introduced appropriate to new contexts, but we are hearing variations on a theme, not a totally new melody. Even when specific leadership functions are described for the first time in the book of Acts or in the epistles, the underlying concepts echo ideas that Jesus had previously introduced to his followers.

The Leader's Perspective

How should an understanding of these biblical images and themes influence leadership behaviour in the church? I would like to propose some ways in which reflection on these topics can shape the leader's perspective of his/her own role, and the place of other believers as followers and potential leaders. In this way I will seek to demonstrate the rationale for studying *all* the biblical terms used for followers of Jesus, rather than simply those that are applied exclusively, or at least primarily, to leaders.

The leader as follower of Jesus

Jesus focused more of his attention on teaching the disciples how to follow than on giving them instructions on how to lead. The single most important lesson for leaders to learn is that they are first sheep, not shepherds;

first children, not fathers or mothers; first imitators, not models. Rather than thinking only about those biblical images that set them apart, leaders should reflect on the many, many more images that apply to them as fully as to any other believer.

Leaders are only a mist, mortal and frail; when they are gone, God will raise up others; there is no place in the church for the building of dynasties, or the creation of celebrities or personality cults. No matter how grand the leader's title, or large his/her responsibility, he/she is still a steward, not an owner; a partner, not an independent contractor; a fellow-worker, not a boss; a member of the body, not the head; a branch of the tree, not the root; a servant, not a master. The common clay pot must not forget that the treasure is *in* the pot, *not* the pot itself.

The leader's view of other followers

Just as leaders ought not to have too high an opinion of themselves, so should they beware of assuming too low an opinion of the other followers of Jesus. Leaders should remember the terms of dignity and honour by which *all* followers of Jesus are described. The people they lead are royal priests, precious treasures, full citizens. They have spiritual gifts that are just as essential to the welfare of the body of Christ as any exercised by the leader. The leader's role is to equip God's people, to empower them, to help them to become as effective as possible in the service of the King. Believers are salt, light, the very aroma of Christ; scattered throughout society in their various vocations, they can become ambassadors and heralds, witnesses and fishers of men.

Many believers have the ability to become teachers and models for younger believers. Some have gifts of administration and leadership that need to be encouraged. Some are still 'newly planted', not yet ready for the responsibilities of leadership – but if given time to mature, they will become able overseers and shepherds.

Many educators have observed that people tend to become what the leader expects them to be. How important it is, therefore, for the church leader to see the other church members as potentially fruitful branches, productive fields, and victorious athletes; as sturdy building blocks, shining stars, and sweet aromas; as beloved brothers and sisters, chosen people, valued fellow-workers, and precious friends. And how essential it is for the leader to help the *people* to see themselves in these terms as well! When leaders respect, honour, recognize, and affirm those they lead, they will find others far more willing to follow them; and when leaders realize the true worth and dignity of those they lead, the leaders themselves will be more ready to lay down their lives in service for those who are so precious to God.

The leader's special role

Yet neither leader nor followers can afford to lose sight of the particular function and calling that is given to the leader. The New Testament writers use special leadership words like *episkopos*, which means one who oversees; *kybernesis*, or the work of piloting a ship; and *hegemonos*, which indicates one who takes charge. One cannot 'go in front' as 'leader' (*prohistamenos*) unless others are willing to follow behind; the shepherd cannot lead the flock to pasture if every sheep wanders off on its own path. There can be no teaching without some who are willing to be instructed, and no mature guidance without others being willing to yield to the wisdom of the elders (*presbyteroi*).

An emphasis on the priesthood of every believer and the importance of every gift can become an excuse for diminished respect for the leadership function. The teaching of the headship of Christ must not become the denial of the legitimacy of any human authority within the church. We are not free to focus only on the images of discipleship which buttress the egalitarian spirit of our age, while rejecting the images that point to the need for authority and submission as essential for both order and forward movement in a loving community.

The Search for Appropriate Images

A question which we must ask continually is whether the images we use, or any of the other symbols we employ, stir the imagination and the feelings of the people to whom we are communicating. Sometimes we need new images to rouse us from our slumber.

The search for appropriate terms and images for church leaders today is complicated by the fact that the more exactly suited a certain image is for a particular time and place, the more difficult it may be to understand it in a different context. How do we speak of precious treasure in fragile clay pots to an aluminium and plastic society? How do we capture the power of the shepherd image with urban youngsters who have never been to a pasture, let alone a zoo, to see a flock of sheep? How meaningful is it to speak of a 'kingdom' to those living under a revolutionary socialist government, or to use the image of a cornerstone with those who construct their homes from mud and thatch? Some might question why we should start with the Bible at all for our imagery, when our own society is twenty centuries and thousands of miles removed.

The most important reason to begin with the biblical imagery is to identify the themes that underlie the images. Those who believe in the full inspiration of Scripture will acknowledge that the images themselves are part of the inspired text, and therefore deserving of our careful study. Once we have identified the basic ideas conveyed by the biblical terms, we can evaluate the extent to which other terms express similar meanings.

For example, we see from a study of the biblical terms that the disciple is one who is under authority. If our own society does not have masters and slaves, there may be other useful images that convey an authority relationship, such as an army recruit with a drill instructor, or a football player with a coach, or a factory worker with a supervisor. To take another illustration, in order to express the idea of the disciple who imitates another, we may explore relationships like the skilled craftsman with the apprentice, or the guru with the follower, or the musician with the young student.

Each image will have its own associations within a given cultural context. Our task is to determine whether the ideas suggested by that image correspond closely enough to the concepts of discipleship and leadership expressed by the biblical metaphors to remain true to scriptural intent.

We would be wise, however, in our search for culturally appropriate terms, to stay close to the biblical images as well. For one thing, the Bible is so full of pictorial and metaphorical language that we cannot teach it adequately without helping people to develop a clear understanding of the biblical images in context. We should not underestimate people's ability to grasp and to apply a biblical image once they have understood its background.

Nor should we overstate our own distance from the biblical images. There are many rural societies in the world today that would have little difficulty understanding the agrarian imagery of the gospels. Modern societies still have athletes, soldiers, children, resident aliens, and ambassadors. People of all places and times understand light, aroma, and the human body; most know the meaning of letters (epistles, written communications), trees, and the functions of planting, watering, and harvesting crops. Some of the biblical images like seal, crown, adoption, priesthood, apostleship, and freeing of slaves require more cultural and historical explanation for full understanding, but many of the terms are quite accessible to the modern reader.

The biblical images and the themes that underlie them should also suggest boundaries which will help us to determine which images are *not* appropriate. Not every first-century term for leader was taken into the Christian vocabulary. Most of the terms associated with the synagogue and pagan religions were avoided. So were the strong authority-laden *arch*-compounds, as well as most other words that denoted ruler and ruled. With images like 'shepherd', which had strong positive associations from the Old Testament writings but unsavoury connotations among the rabbis (who scorned shepherds as unreliable and dishonest), the biblical writers chose the particular aspects of the image that they wanted to emphasize. Perhaps a similar evaluation could be performed with words that may carry either positive or negative connotations when applied to leaders in a Christian community – words like 'manager' in industrialized societies, and 'guru' in a south Asian context.

The Development of Leaders

A study of the biblical images can help present-day leaders of the church to examine their ideas, their attitudes, and their patterns of behaviour. Such a study can also suggest directions for the development of future leaders. How shall we follow in the footsteps of Jesus to nurture leaders for the church of tomorrow?

In the first place, we must develop leaders who have learned how to follow, who see themselves as lifelong students and servants of the Master. Unless one can accept direction cheerfully, one is not ready to give direction to others. Leadership training begins with obeying the order to leave our nets and cheerfully picking up fragments of food in baskets; it involves patiently lingering to attend to the sick, staying awake for prayer, and humbly washing feet. Leadership training should not be connected with elitism and special privilege, but with harder work, greater discipline, and more sacrificial service.

Secondly, leadership training should provide instruction within the context of personal apprenticeship. To be a follower of Jesus is to learn a pattern of life, not simply to give assent to a creed. Such training in attitudes and behaviour cannot possibly occur in a classroom setting alone. There must be opportunities for leaders to live, eat, work, travel, serve, and share with emergent leaders. A life that is not observed cannot be imitated.

Third, the development of leaders needs to involve them in commitment to a community as well as to training for a task. The emergent leaders must learn to function effectively as members of a team. They must learn to love their fellow-believers, including other leaders, as members of one family. They must come to rejoice and to suffer with the other members of the body, and to respect the contribution of their fellow-workers.

Fourth, the spiritual aspects of leadership must be stressed. More and more tools of management, planning, and organization are available today. But there is a crying need for leaders who will pray fervently, love deeply, and wage spiritual warfare courageously. Leaders need to be schooled in faith, learning total dependence on the Lord as branches of the vine and members drawing life from the head. They must learn that however much they plant or water, God causes the growth, that he is Lord of the harvest. They must be determined to spread the light and aroma of Christ, not to become well-known themselves. Their message must be delivered as faithful ambassadors and heralds, communicating the words given to them by God's Word and Spirit, not depending on their own intellect or eloquence. In short, they must believe that Christ is everything – *everything* – and that apart from him, they can do nothing (Jn. 15:5).

Yet the ministry of leadership today takes place in a world that is increasingly urban, international, complex and technologically sophisticated. The leader is called to be a steward, a wise manager of all of God's resources – which may include accounting procedures, mass media, computer technology, staff and volunteers with specialized training, and greatly increased knowledge about organizational functioning and cross-cultural communication. Leadership training must include orientation to as much of this modern knowledge and technique as is necessary to foster good stewardship of God's resources. Any tool can be useful in the hands of God's steward, as long as the tool remains the servant and does not become the master.

Some Final Thoughts

Images, or metaphors, are powerful. They shape what we see, by highlighting certain features and moving others into the background. They dominate our patterns of analysis and reflection. They suggest explanations as to why we relate to one another the way we do, or why certain structures exist. They support particular understandings of the past, interpretations of the present, and scenarios for the future. They promote some values and discourage others. They suggest priorities and awaken emotions.

The choice to emphasize a given metaphor and to put aside another can set the direction of a community and its leadership. Therefore, we must become aware of the images we use, and how we are using them. In particular, we must examine the metaphors we use in the development of our future leaders. For example, what is the balance between our use of 'task' metaphors and our use of 'relationship' metaphors? To what extent do our images reinforce in our future leaders a sense of accountability to God? Do they think of themselves first as 'brothers/sisters' and as 'servants', or as rulers and bosses? Do they speak of their relationships to others more in terms of 'among' and 'under', or in terms of 'over'? Do they understand that there *are* legitimate differences in responsibility and authority that can be assigned within the community? Or does their emphasis on equality for all in the fellowship blind them to their own need to be willing to come under the authority of a fellow-servant, or perhaps to *exercise* authority as a fellow-servant?

Our answers to questions like these today will determine the shape of the church in which we serve tomorrow.

A

ALIEN, RESIDENT (see also RESIDENT, TEMPORARY)

The resident alien (*paroikos*, a compound of *para*, 'by', and *oikos*, 'house') is a long-term resident of the community who enjoys its protection yet lacks the rights of a citizen. This term is introduced in 1 Peter 1:17: 'Live your lives as strangers (*tes paroikias*) here in reverent fear.'

The resident alien has a different culture, speaks a different language, follows a different religion, practises different customs. People know that the resident alien does not share their roots and does not really belong. Because of these differences, the resident alien may arouse curiosity or suspicion and may suffer discrimination and social barriers.

In the first century, resident aliens were unable to vote, own land, hold priestly offices or the primary public offices, receive certain public honours, or intermarry with full citizens. Although resident aliens received only partial legal protection, they were fully liable for military service, production quotas, and taxes. Because of these restrictions, their opportunities for social or economic advancement were quite limited.

In 1 Peter 2:11, Peter uses this term to exhort his readers to distinctive, holy living: 'Dear friends, I urge you as aliens (*paroikous*) and strangers in the world, to abstain from sinful desires, which war against your soul.' Since the real home of Christians is elsewhere, Peter warns them against conformity to the patterns of this world.

Outside of 1 Peter, this image occurs in one other place. In Ephesians 2:19, Paul says to the Gentiles: 'You are no longer foreigners and aliens (*paroikoi*), but fellow-citizens with God's people and members of God's household.' Here the image is reversed – the Gentile believers are not seen as aliens, but as 'no longer aliens'. It all depends on the point of reference.

AMBASSADOR

In 2 Corinthians 5:20, Paul writes: 'We are therefore Christ's ambassadors, as though God were making his appeal through us.' The 'ambassador' (expressed through the verb *presbeuo*, to be an ambassador, or to work as an ambassador) is an authorized representative, who represents the people who send him and negotiates for them. The ambassador doesn't just deliver the message – he also takes action on behalf of the sender.

In Ephesians 6, Paul invites the Corinthians to pray that he will be able to proclaim boldly the gospel, 'for which I am an ambassador in chains' (v. 20). As a prisoner in Rome, to which foreign delegates came from far and wide, Paul thinks of himself as an ambassador from the King of Kings. The status of the ambassador is generally related to the status of the ruler that he represents. This high honour is therefore a privilege available to the humblest of willing believers.

APOSTLE

The word 'apostle' (transliteration of *apostolos*), is based on the verb 'to send' (*apostello*). The verb appears frequently in the gospels, in reference to the sending of Jesus by the Father (e.g. Mt. 15:24; Jn. 5:36), and the sending of the disciples by Jesus (e.g. Mt. 10:5; Jn. 17:18). Jesus also uses the verb often in his parables to describe servants sent on assignments by their masters (e.g. Mt. 20:2; Mk. 12:1–6).

But the noun 'apostle', referring to the messenger who is sent, occurs only a handful of times in the gospels, most often in Luke, usually as a designation for the twelve disciples. On two occasions, however, Jesus uses the word *apostolos* in reference to his followers. The first instance is the appointment of the twelve, recorded in Mark 3:13–19 and Luke 6:12–16. The importance of this occasion is emphasized by Luke's observation that Jesus spent the whole night beforehand in prayer. When morning came, Luke tells us, 'he called his disciples to him and chose twelve of them, whom he also designated apostles' (6:13). Then, in both Mark and Luke, comes the listing of the twelve names.

The initiative of Jesus in this whole process is evident. The apostles were not volunteers. Jesus chose the time. Jesus chose the place. Not all of the followers of Jesus were included in the choice. Rather, Mark says explicitly that Jesus 'called to him *those he wanted*, and they came to him' (3:13; emphasis mine). All were invited to follow Jesus, and to listen to his teachings; but not all were invited to be part of the inner circle who would be 'with him' and who would be sent out 'to preach and to have authority to drive out demons' (Mk. 3:14,15). It was only these twelve, selected and gathered by Jesus' deliberate choice, who would enter into the more intensive course of leadership development, and whom Jesus would designate as apostles (Lk. 6:13).

To emphasize this act of narrowing and selecting, Luke notes that Jesus chose 'from them,' that is, from the larger group of disciples. Thus not every disciple is described by the term 'apostle'. There are some roles in the community of Jesus which are 'by invitation only'. The selection appears to have taken place in full view of the other disciples, not in some secret ceremony of initiation. Thus the special leadership role of these twelve would have been clearly underscored in the eyes of the entire group of Jesus' followers.

The authority of Jesus over these twelve is also implied in the act of naming: Simon he nicknamed 'Peter', the rock, and James and John he designated as the 'sons of thunder'.

The 'sent ones' would have two basic responsibilities. First, they were called together to be *with* Jesus, that is, to share a common life, to enter into a personal relationship with him and with one another. In the second place, they were called to share in a task, to announce a message and to exercise authority over the powers of darkness. They would share in the divine authority. Their influence would be more than mere moral persuasion; rather they were authorized to speak and to take action as representatives of the Messiah himself.

The one other occasion in the gospels where Jesus uses the noun *apostolos* is in John 13:14–16, just after he has washed the disciples' feet. He tells them:

Now that I, your Lord and Teacher, have washed your feet, you also should wash one another's feet. I have set you an example that you should do as I have done for you. I tell you the truth, no servant is greater than his master, nor is a messenger (*apostolos*) greater than the one who sent him.

Jesus has clearly stated his own position of leadership. He is the Lord, the one who holds the authority, and he is the teacher, the one who has the knowledge. But he has set an example of service of the lowliest kind. What is demonstrated by the greater can certainly be expected from the lesser. Therefore the disciples are obligated to do for one another what Jesus has done for them.

Jesus supports his point by arguing that the servant is 'not greater' than his master – in other words, the servant is commonly acknowledged to be less than his master. For a servant to say that certain work is beneath his dignity would be to imply that he has greater status than his master. Similarly, says Jesus, the messenger, or apostle (Jesus is speaking in generic terms of one who is sent by another, not specifically of the twelve), is not greater than the one who sent him.

When Jesus first designated the twelve as apostles, there was an emphasis on the special privileges of intimacy with Jesus and participation in his mission that they would enjoy. They would share in his authority as proclaimers of the divine word and conquerors of demons. But here Jesus reminds them that no matter how much authority the 'apostle' may have, he remains one who has been sent by another. His authority does not come from himself, but from the one who sent him.

It would have been very easy for the apostles to focus on those whom they were *greater than*, rather than to remember that they themselves were under authority, and were not independent agents. In John 13, the sentence structure of verse 16 clearly puts the 'messenger' (*apostolos*) parallel with 'servant', and the sender with the master, thus emphasizing that to be an apostle is first to be a servant.

Yet in the very next verses of John 13 Jesus returns to the theme of the high status and privilege of the one who is sent. In verse 18 he reminds the disciples that he has chosen them, that they are in this circle by his initiative, not their own. But in verse 20 he says: 'I tell you the truth, whoever accepts anyone I send accepts me; and whoever accepts me accepts the one who sent me.' Jesus' reference to the Father's sending recalls the phrase at the beginning of the passage (13:3) where John states that Jesus knew that 'he had come from God'. So then Jesus himself has been sent by God, a position of high authority and privilege, yet he stoops to wash feet. Similarly the disciples are privileged to be sent into the world as messengers, apostles, of Jesus. The one who welcomes them welcomes the Son of God. Yet the apostles, like the one who sent them, are called to serve in humility.

Outside of the gospels, most of the occurrences of 'apostle' refer explicitly to the twelve (e.g. Acts 1:2,26; 6:2; 8:1), and to the apostle Paul (e.g. Rom. 1:1; 11:13), who received his special call from the risen Jesus on the road to Damascus. However, the circle of reference is also enlarged to include Barnabas (Acts 14:4,14), Silas and Timothy (1 Thess. 1:1; 2:6,7), and possibly Andronicus and Junias (Rom. 16:7).[1]

---

[1] Depending on whether the phrase 'outstanding among the apostles' means that these individuals were outstanding *as* apostles, or whether they were considered to be outstanding by the circle of the apostles. The latter explanation seems more likely, in that Paul's approach is not to hold one leader in greater esteem than the rest (cf. his references to 'those who seemed to be important' in Galatians 2:2,6).

Several passages refer to the group of apostles in a general sense, as a class of leaders within the church. In 1 Corinthians 12:28,29, the apostles are listed first among the spiritual gifts. Similarly, in Ephesians 4:11,12 they are cited first among those who were given by Christ to the church in order to 'prepare God's people for works of service'. In Ephesians 3:5, Paul says that the mystery of Christ has been revealed by the Spirit to 'God's holy apostles and prophets'.

A related word, 'apostleship' (*apostoles*) is introduced in Acts and the letters. In each case it refers to the person who has received authoritative commissioning by Jesus. The first followers of Jesus in Jerusalem pray for wisdom to select an individual to fill Judas' vacancy in 'this apostolic ministry (*apostoles*)' (Acts 1:25). In his letter to the Romans, having introduced himself as one 'called to be an apostle' (1:1), Paul says that he has received 'grace and apostleship' (1:5) to call the Gentiles to faith in Christ. To the Corinthians, who questioned his credentials, Paul insisted, 'You are the seal of my apostleship in the Lord' (1 Cor. 9:2).

The ministry of apostle is not one for which a person volunteers. Rather, Paul's emphasis is on being called to be an apostle (Rom. 1:1; 1 Cor. 1:1), being appointed as an apostle (1 Tim. 2:7; 2 Tim. 1:11), and being an apostle by the will of God (2 Tim. 1:1) and at the command of God (1 Tim. 1:1). God is the one who commissions authoritative leaders for his church; they do not appoint themselves.

To be an apostle is to suffer. Paul compares the apostles to gladiators brought last into the arena to fight to the death (1 Cor. 4:9ff). Leadership in Christ's church is not a position of luxury and ease, but the privilege of leading the way into suffering – to be the first to die, to be made a spectacle, to be seen as weak, foolish, and dishonoured in the eyes of the world.

The true apostle is known not only by his willingness to suffer (cf. 2 Cor. 11), but by a number of other authenticating marks. The apostle has seen the risen Lord (1 Cor. 9:1; 15:7–9; Acts 1:21,22). The proof of his ministry can be seen in unbelievers converted and churches established (1 Cor. 9:1,2). He performs signs, wonders, and miracles in the power of the Spirit (2 Cor. 12:12). When the later letters of the New Testament speak of the apostles, they refer to those who laid the foundations in the early days of the church (Eph. 2:20; 2 Pet. 3:2; Jude 17; Rev. 21:14). Although there are functions in the church today which parallel the first-century apostles' work of church-planting and pioneering in new areas, the New Testament usage of the term seems generally to focus on a specific group of early leaders who had no successors in the strict sense.

Even if the apostolic office in the strict New Testament sense has not existed since the first century, the apostolic function of opening new territories for the gospel and planting new churches among previously unreached peoples is certainly continuing. Whether or not we accept such a flexible, informal definition of 'apostle', it is clear that 'apostle' is not one of those terms that is, or should, be applied to every follower of Jesus. Rather, it describes a particular initiating leadership role, a specific pioneering function, as well as a distinctive divine calling, which go beyond the general command for every disciple to bear witness to Jesus.

AROMA

In 2 Corinthians 2, Paul describes the Christian life in terms of the triumphal procession of a victorious general, accompanied by the burning of aromatic spices. The bystanders have two very different reactions to the aroma. Some find it pleasing and life-giving; others find it nauseating and deadly. Paul uses two words for odour – 'fragrance' (*euodia*) and 'aroma' (*osme*), which can be either positive or negative. He says:

> But thanks be to God, who always leads us in triumphal procession in Christ and through us spreads everywhere the fragrance (*osmen*) of the knowledge of him. For we are to God the aroma (*euodia*) of Christ among those who are being saved and those who are perishing. To the one we are the smell (*osme*) of death; to the other, the fragrance (*osme*) of life (2:14–16).

Fragrances convey powerful associations; they have the ability to awaken memories and emotions. Odours are also pervasive. Just as the fragrance of the ointment poured on Jesus' feet filled the house (Jn. 12:3), so the fragrance from the procession penetrates 'everywhere' (2 Cor. 2:14). Whether it is perceived as pleasant or repulsive, the odour cannot be ignored. In the same way, the Christian witness in the world will provoke a variety of responses, but if it is truly the 'fragrance of Christ', people will be unable to disregard it.

ATHLETE (see also BOXER, RUNNER, WRESTLER)

Even though terms related to athletics were not used by Jesus, they became very popular in the writings of the early church, starting with the writings of the apostle Paul, who spent much of his time ministering in Hellenistic cities where the stadium was one of the most prominent and popular public places, and where the gymnasiums were filled with young people exercising and receiving instruction.

Of the various athletically-oriented words, the most general term is the verb 'contend' (*athleo*), which means to compete in an athletic contest in the arena. Paul urges the Philippians to stand firm in one spirit, 'contending as one man (*synathlountes*) for the faith of the gospel' (Phil. 1:27). His expression evokes the image of an athletic team, a group with a common goal and a common opponent, whose victory depends not just on individual performance but on co-ordination of effort. Paul uses the same word later in his letter when he pleads for Euodia and Syntyche to live in harmony with one another, reminding them that they have 'contended at my side (*synathlesan*) in the cause of the gospel' (Phil. 4:3). These two women had forgotten that they were teammates and had started to treat one another as opponents and competitors. They had lost sight of the real enemy.

In 2 Timothy 2:5, Paul uses the image of the athlete to motivate Timothy to accept the disciplines that are needed to ensure victory: 'Similarly, if anyone competes as an athlete (*athlei*), he does not receive the victor's crown unless he competes (*athlesei*) according to the rules.' The author of Hebrews uses the related noun 'contest' (*athlesis*): 'Remember those earlier days after you had received the light, when you stood your ground in a great contest (*athlesin*) in the face of suffering' (10:32).

This dimension of struggle implied in the athletic contest becomes even more focused in another Greek word translated as 'contend' or 'struggle' (*agonizo*) and the related noun 'contest' (*agon*). Paul encourages the Philippians who have suffered through the same struggle (*agona*) that he himself has had with those who oppose the gospel (Phil. 1:30). At Thessalonica, as in Macedonia, Paul experienced the same strong opposition (*agoni*, 1 Thess. 2:2). He urges Timothy to 'fight the good fight (*agona*) of the faith' (1 Tim. 6:12), and expresses confidence that he, Paul, has already 'fought the good fight (*agona agonismai*)' (2 Tim. 4:7). Paul speaks of struggling (*agonizomenos*) with all his energy to help believers to become mature in Christ (Col. 1:29), and, again, of struggling (*agona*) for their unity, encouragement, and understanding (Col. 2:1,2). At the end of the same letter he commends Epaphras as one who is 'always wrestling (*agonizomenos*) in prayer for you' (4:12). The author of Hebrews exhorts his readers to run with perseverance 'the race (*agona*)' marked out for them (12:1).

So, then, the image of the contest implies opposition, suffering, and hardship. It speaks of the need for endurance and the willingness to bear pain if the goal is to be achieved. It also implies discipline and the willingness to sacrifice personal comfort and short-term gratification for the sake of long-term goals. Paul reminds the Corinthians that 'Everyone who competes in the games (*agonizomenos*) goes into strict training' (1 Cor. 9:25). The contest imagery reminds us that we are in a battle where there are winners as well as losers. The struggle is not against fellow-Christians, but against the forces of darkness that oppose the gospel.

Although the image of the contest can be used in association with athletic events like races (e.g. 1 Cor. 9:24,26; Heb. 12:1), the primary reference is to combat sports like wrestling and boxing, which played such a prominent part in the Greek athletic contests. That is why the reference to Epaphras' struggle in prayer in Colossians 4:12 is translated by the NIV as 'wrestling'.

Through the athletic images of the New Testament (cf. boxer, runner, wrestler) run several themes. First is that the Christian life requires effort and exertion – simply to keep moving forward, let alone to complete the task; it is not going to be easy; there will be pain and suffering, even the shedding of blood and possibly the loss of life. Second, there are disciplines to observe and rules to keep, just as an athlete has in both training and competition. Third, there will be opposition; the chief opponent is the devil, who is not just a competitor but a deadly enemy. Fourth, there is a goal to be attained which will make all the sacrifices worthwhile. And fifth, the Christian does not struggle alone; he or she is part of a team striving together to achieve what they could never attain independently.

B

BABY (see also CHILD)

'Baby' (*brephos*) is used by Luke to describe Elizabeth's unborn child (Lk. 1:41,44), the newborn Jesus (Lk. 2:12,16), and the children brought to Jesus for blessing (Lk. 18:15). This is the word chosen by Peter in his exhortation to new Christians: 'Like newborn babies (*brephe*), crave pure spiritual milk, so that by it you may grow up in your salvation' (1 Pet. 2:2). Unlike the word 'infant' (*nepios*), more often used to describe immature Christians, the reference to 'babies' in this passage conveys no tone of rebuke.

BATCH OF DOUGH

In 1 Corinthians 5 Paul appeals to the congregation to deal firmly with the sin that has been tolerated openly among them, so that the problems do not become even more widespread. He says: 'Don't you know that a little yeast works through the whole batch of dough (*phyrama*)? Get rid of the old yeast that you may be a new batch (*phyrama*) without yeast – as you really are' (vv. 6,7). The members of the church are so connected to one another that the sin in the life of one can soon spread to become sin in the life of many. Impurity in a part can endanger the integrity of the whole. The interrelatedness of the community of believers is a great strength, but it also opens the community to great risk.

BELIEVER

One of the most commonly used terms for followers of Jesus, especially on the part of Luke and Paul, is 'believers' (*pisteuontes* or *pistoi*). Luke uses these words many times in Acts in general reference to followers of Jesus, whether Jew or Gentile (2:44; 4:32; 10:45; 15:5; 16:1; 19:18; 21:20,25; 22:19). Paul uses the terms frequently in his letters as well (1 Cor. 14:22; 2 Cor. 6:15; Eph. 1:1,19; 1 Thess. 1:7; 2 Thess. 1:10; 1 Tim. 4:10; 5:16).

The verbal form (*pisteuontes*) indicates that believing in Jesus is an ongoing state of trust and commitment. The noun form (*pistoi*) indicates the solid commitment of faith which describes these individuals. In both cases the object of faith is the gospel, and more particularly, Jesus Christ himself. As Paul and Silas said to the Philippian jailer, 'Believe in the Lord Jesus, and you will be saved – you and your household' (Acts 16:31). The distinguishing mark of the Christian is that he or she is a believer; it is this faith which ties Jews and Gentiles together, and which divides those who are truly in the church from those who are not. Belief in Jesus Christ forms the common bond which makes possible the remarkable sharing seen in Acts 2:44 and 4:32.

It is what delivers us from the kingdom of darkness and ushers us into the kingdom of light (Acts 19:18; cf. 2 Cor. 6:15, 1 Tim. 4:10). Faith is the distinguishing mark which causes some to be persecuted while others are left alone (Acts 22:19). It qualifies us to experience the resurrection power of Christ (Eph. 1:19). No term more fully captures what it is to be a Christian.

BELOVED

'Beloved' (*agapetos*) is an affectionate term of address, used often in the New Testament letters, and sometimes found in combination with other terms like 'children' and 'brothers'. Since Jesus had said that the distinctive mark of his community of disciples would be their love for one another (Jn. 13:34,35), it is not surprising to find this word used so frequently in their communication with one another. This term emphasizes that the church is not simply a group of co-workers or fellow-pilgrims, drawn together by a common task and destination; it is also knit together at the level of affections.

Every one of the New Testament letter writers, except for James, uses this affectionate term.[1] John uses 'beloved' six times in the five short chapters of his first letter. Thus the relationship of these spiritual leaders to the congregations to which they wrote, with whatever authority they exercised, was based on love. As Jesus explained in John

---

[1] Thus Paul (1 Cor. 10:14; 2 Cor. 7:1; 12:19; Phil. 2:12; 4:1; Col. 4:14; Philem. 1); Peter (1 Pet. 2:11; 4:12; 2 Pet. 3:1,8,14,17); the author of Hebrews (6:9); Jude (vv. 3,17,20); and John (1 Jn. 2:7; 3:2,21; 4:1,7,11; 2 Jn. 1,2,5,11).

10, the difference between the Good Shepherd and the hired hand is found in the loving concern that the shepherd bears for the sheep.

The same word used for the believers' love for one another is also used by Paul of God's love for the believer. He addresses his readers in Romans 1:7: 'To all in Rome who are loved (*agapetois*) by God,' and exhorts the Colossian Christians: 'as God's chosen people, holy and dearly loved (*egapemenoi*)' (3:12). Therefore, in loving one another we are loving those on whom God has already set *his* love.

BODY, MEMBER OF

One of the best-known and widely used images of the church introduced by the apostle Paul is that of the 'body' (*soma*) and its members (*mele*). Although he develops the image at some length in Romans 12, 1 Corinthians 12, Ephesians 4, and several passages in Colossians, Paul is the only New Testament writer who uses it. In three of the passages, the references to the body are linked with discussion of spiritual gifts. In Romans 12, following the exhortation to Christians to surrender their bodies to God as living sacrifices, Paul gives a concise summary of this aspect of the body image:

> Just as each of us has one body (*somati*) with many members (*mele*), and these members do not all have the same function, so in Christ we who are many form one body, and each member belongs to all the others. We have different gifts, according to the grace given us (12:4–6).

Several features of the body image are evident in these verses. First, the body consists of those who are 'in Christ';

their relationship to him makes them part of the body. Second, there is only one body; each individual member is in some way identified with and connected to the one body. Third, the body is very diverse; it is comprised of many different parts. Fourth, these different parts have special capacities, spiritual gifts, which are intended to be used for the welfare of the body and to enable the body to perform the functions for which it was designed. Fifth, the parts of the body are interdependent; they comprise a system; each part can function properly only as it operates in co-ordination with the whole.

These same basic features can be seen in the other passages where spiritual gifts and the body are discussed. In 1 Corinthians 12, Paul states that the body is a unit, even though there are many parts (vv. 12,20). The body is comprised of those who are part of Christ (vv. 12,27), who have been baptized by his Spirit (v. 13). Each different function is essential to the welfare of the body (vv. 14–25). The parts are interconnected such that the experience of the part affects the whole; they suffer together and rejoice together (v. 26).

In Ephesians 4, Paul again stresses the oneness of the body (v. 4), based on its vital union with Christ, who is the source of life and growth (vv. 15,16). Each part has essential work to do (v. 16). The purpose of the spiritual gifts of apostle, prophet, evangelist, and pastor-teacher is to prepare God's people for service, in order to contribute to the building up of the body toward unity, knowledge, and maturity (vv. 11–13). The oneness of the body is also expressed in 1 Corinthians 10:17, in the context of instructions about the Lord's Supper: 'Because there is one loaf, we, who are many, are one body, for we all partake of the one loaf.'

The intimate connection of the parts of the body to one another is the basis for Paul's exhortation to truthfulness in Ephesians 4:25: 'Each of you must put off falsehood and speak truthfully to his neighbour, for we are all members of one body.' This connectedness is also the ground of the appeal for peace in Colossians 3:15: 'Let the peace of Christ rule in your hearts, since as members of one body you were called to peace.' Because believers are in fact connected to one another through their common participation in Christ, they must do nothing that would tend to drive a wedge between them.

In his discussion of the new oneness that Christ has made possible between Jews and Gentiles, Paul says that God has created 'one new man', reconciling them both to God 'in this one body' (Eph. 2:15,16), a reference both to Christ's body tortured on the cross and to the new fact of union in the community of Christ. Then in the next chapter he speaks of the 'mystery' that Gentiles and Jews are 'members together of one body (*syssoma*)' (3:6).

One primary theme, then, of the body metaphor is unity in diversity. But another recurrent aspect of this image is the vital connection of the believers individually as well as corporately to Christ, who is the head of the body. In Ephesians 1:22,23, Paul says that God appointed Christ to be 'head over everything for the church, which is his body', placing him above every rule and authority, and putting all things under his feet. The image of headship in this context is plainly one of rule and authority. Christ is head over everything, not just the church.

Other passages focus on Christ's headship over the church in particular. Ephesians 4:15,16 speaks of growing up into Christ, who is the head, from whom the whole body grows; here the head is the source of growth. In

Ephesians 5, where Paul calls wives to submit to their husbands, that is, to come willingly under their authority, he grounds his exhortation in the observation that 'the husband is the head of the wife as Christ is the head of the church, his body, of which he is the Saviour' (v. 23). In view of the parallel between these sections and the ones that follow concerning parents with children (6:1–4), and masters with slaves (6:5–9), it is clear that headship here again is an image of authority.

But later in the passage about husbands and wives, Paul draws out another implication of the body metaphor in our relationship to Christ – that Christ feeds and cares for his church, just as a person does his own body (5:29). Paul also points to the parallels between Christ's loving sacrifice for the church, and the selfless love which husbands are to show to their wives (5:25–28,33). Thus the authority which Christ possesses as head is exercised in love, for the benefit of the members of the body.

In the book of Colossians, in a section on the supremacy of Christ over the whole created order, Paul again speaks of Christ as the 'head of the body, the church' (1:18), and as the 'head over every power and authority' (2:10). He describes the false teacher as one who has 'lost connection with the Head, from whom the whole body, supported and held together by its ligaments and sinews, grows as God causes it to grow' (2:19).

The image of the body with Christ as its head thus stresses the total authority of Christ in the community of disciples and the total dependence of the disciples on Christ for life and growth. The headship of Christ also puts human leadership in right perspective, for no human being is ever called 'head' of the church; Christ is the authority to whom all human leaders are responsible.

BOXER (see also ATHLETE, WRESTLER)

Paul uses words from combat sports like wrestling and boxing in his description of the struggle and disciplines of the Christian life. In 1 Corinthians 9:26 he employs the image of the boxer, saying, 'I do not fight (i.e. "box", *pykteuo*) like a man beating the air.' His action is purposeful, intent on victory.

BRANCH (OF VINE)

In John 15:1 Jesus says, 'I am the true vine (*ampelos*)', comparing his disciples to branches (*klemata*). This is the only occurrence of this metaphor in the gospels, or anywhere else in the New Testament. Yet its placement in the upper room discourse, and the number of verses given to the development of the illustration, testify to its importance.

Two kinds of branches are contrasted here – those that bear fruit and those that do not. The unfruitful branches are cut off; after they are thrown away they wither and are burned. In contrast, the fruitful branches are cut only partially, in order to prune them, so that they will bear even more fruit. In both cases parts are amputated; yet in the first instance the branch is *removed*, whereas in the second instance it is *improved*.

The branch derives its life only through remaining in the vine, which is its sole source of productivity. The branch has no vitality in itself. In the same way, says Jesus, the disciple's growth and influence depend entirely on his union with Christ. The product of his life, whether in development of godly character or in impact on the lives of others, derives solely from his vital relationship with the Master. The proof of genuine discipleship is found in the production of abundant fruit, the result of consistent dependence on Jesus the true vine.

BRANCHES (OF OLIVE TREE)

As with the image of the body, the olive tree (*elaia*) is a living organism, and conveys the idea of unity in the midst of diversity. In Romans 11:16–24 Paul employs an extended metaphor, describing the people of God as a cultivated olive tree whose branches are broken off so that wild shoots can be grafted in. The roots of the tree are the patriarchs; the cultivated tree is the Jews; and the wild olive is the Gentiles. Because of unbelief, branches are broken off, whether natural or grafted; and by belief, both can be grafted in again. So then, the church as a whole grows together as one tree, but the only basis for being included, as well as for continuing, is faith, not any natural merit. This image highlights the gracious action of God, as well as the active human response of faith, in the formation of the believing community.

BROTHER / SISTER

In terms of the sheer number of occurrences, one of the terms used most frequently by Jesus is 'brother' (*adelphos*). It appears several times in the Sermon on the Mount, in the sections on anger and reconciliation ('if anyone is angry with his brother . . . your brother has something against you . . . be reconciled to your brother' Mt. 5:21–24), love for enemies ('if you greet only your brothers' Mt. 5:43–48), and judging others ('. . . the speck of sawdust in your brother's eye . . . How can you say to your brother . . . remove the speck from your brother's eye' 7:1–5; cf. Lk. 6:41,42). Then in Matthew 18:15–35, Jesus teaches his disciples about how to respond to the 'brother' who sins against them, and who needs to be forgiven again and again.

In each case Jesus introduces the term in the context of interpersonal tension. The explosion of anger, the long bitter grudge, the perception of a defect in the other, the suffering of a personal injury – each tempt us to maintain distance between ourselves and the other person. Yet in these very situations, Jesus reminds his disciples that they are connected to one another; they are members of a family, they are brothers. They cannot separate themselves from one another any more than they can cancel the bonds that tie them to their own families. It is true that those who are closest to them can hurt them most deeply, and will probably hurt them most often. But Jesus reminds his disciples that they remain brothers, and must seek reconciliation.

The word 'brother' is primarily a reciprocal word, a description of an egalitarian relationship. Brothers are fundamentally peers. Yet the brother relationship among the disciples does not remove the possibility for discipline or the exercise of authority within their community. In Matthew 18 Jesus insists that the brother who sins must be disciplined strongly if he refuses to listen to admonition; if he persists, he will be excommunicated, treated like an outsider, expelled from the fellowship. Yet, Jesus says in a similar passage in Luke 17:3, if there is repentance, the brother must be forgiven. There is a fundamental bond that remains and must be restored.

The egalitarian implications of the word 'brother' are highlighted in Matthew 23, in the passage where Jesus is rebuking the hypocrisy of the status-seeking Pharisees, with their love for prominent positions and distinctive titles. Jesus specifically warns his disciples: 'You are not to be called "Rabbi", for you have only one Master and you are all brothers' (23:8). In the preceding verses Jesus criticizes the Pharisees for doing everything for show. They do not practise what they preach; they burden others, but give no help in lifting those burdens; they do everything for people to see; they love places of honour at the banquets and the most important seats in the synagogues; they yearn to be recognized in public places and to have people address them with honorific titles. All of these practices feed their pride, their sense of being separate from and above the people. They do not want to be seen as 'among', but 'over'.

But the disciples of Jesus must not imitate these errors. They are, Jesus reminds them, brothers first of all. They are not 'over' but 'among'. And they are also 'under'. They have one Master/teacher, one Father in heaven, and one teacher/leader (Mt. 23:8–10). The image of 'brother' is introduced to emphasize that the disciples are all on the same level ground, all equally responsible to God as Father.

The use of the word 'brother' implies the recognition of a bond. In the parable of the sheep and the goats, the King rewards the righteous because 'whatever you did for one of the least of these brothers of mine, you did for me' (Mt. 25:40). Whoever is called the King's brother is identified with the King in the closest possible way.

Even when Jesus predicts Peter's denial, he encourages Peter by telling him: 'When you have turned back, strengthen your brothers' (Lk. 22:32). Jesus knows that after such a tragic failure, Peter will not feel very much like a part of the community; yet he remains a brother among brothers. Similarly, after his resurrection appearance to the women, Jesus says, 'Go and tell my brothers to go to Galilee' (Mt. 28:10; cf. Jn. 20:17). These are warm words, spoken in a context where the disciples might have felt ashamed and distant from Jesus, because they had all deserted him at the time of his arrest. But Jesus moves to close the gap by the use of the term 'brother'. In so doing, he reminds the disciples that they are not only brothers of one another, but also brothers to *him*.

When his own natural family wanted to see him, Jesus replied that 'whoever does the will of my Father in heaven is my brother (*adelphos*) and sister (*adelphe*) and mother' (Mt. 12:48–50; cf. Mk. 3:33–35; and Lk. 8:19–21). That is, those who obey and trust God are included in a new spiritual family, with bonds that are even more fundamental and enduring than those that tie individuals together in biological families. The word 'brother' implies personal relationship to Jesus and to the community of faith. Jesus' lack of deference to his natural family members is more understandable in the light of the information provided in Mark 3:21, where we learn that Jesus' family had gone to take charge of him, because they were convinced that he was out of his mind. Yet in a kinship-oriented society like Israel, still it must have been startling for people to hear of a bond that was even deeper than that of the natural family.

Notice that though the relationship between Jesus and the disciple is initiated by Jesus, it is cemented and confirmed by the willing response of the follower; only the ones who do the will of the Father (Mt. 12:50; Mk. 3:35), who hear God's word and put it into practice (Lk. 8:21) are included in the circle of Jesus' brothers and sisters.

Some form of the word 'brother' (*adelphos*) is found in every New Testament book except Titus and Jude. From Acts through Revelation, fellow-Christians are called 'brother' over two hundred times and 'sister' several times as well. Sometimes the reference is to individuals (e.g. 'our sister Phoebe', Rom. 16:1; 'Tychicus the dear brother', Eph. 6:21). Timothy is called 'brother' five times, four times by Paul (2 Cor. 1:1; Col. 1:1; 1 Thess. 3:2; Philem. 1) and once by the author of Hebrews (13:23). Twice in his first letter Peter refers to the community of believers as 'the brotherhood (*adelphotes*)' (1 Pet. 2:17; 5:9).

Even the leading apostles are called 'brother', such as Paul (by Ananias in Acts 9:17 and 22:13; by the Jerusalem elders in Acts 21:20, and by Peter, in 2 Peter 3:15); and John (referring to himself, in Revelation 1:9).[2] In Acts 15, two verses underscore that the leader is also a brother: Judas and Silas are called 'leaders among the brothers' (15:22), and the letter to the Gentile Christians is addressed from 'the apostles and elders, your brothers' (15:23). Thus a community of brothers and sisters can still have leaders, and those who are leaders nevertheless remain brethren. The equality of status implied in the term 'brother' does not preclude differences in leadership roles.

Sometimes the term 'brother' or 'sister' is used in a general sense to denote 'fellow-Christian' ('Suppose a brother or sister is without clothes', Jas. 2:15; cf. Rom.

---

[2] Others so designated include Quartus (Rom. 16:24), Sosthenes (1 Cor. 1:1), Apollos (1 Cor. 16:12), Titus (2 Cor. 2:13), Tychicus (Eph. 6:21 and Col. 4:7), Epaphroditus (Phil. 2:25), Onesimus (Col. 4:9), Apphia ('our sister', Philem. 2), Philemon (Philem. 7,20), Silas (1 Pet. 5:12), and two unnamed individuals (2 Cor. 8:18,22).

14:10; 1 Cor. 7:12; 1 Thess. 4:6; 1 Jn. 2:9). Other times 'brother' refers to the whole group of Christians in a given locality: 'Peter stood up among the brothers' (Acts 1:15); 'All the brothers greet you' (1 Cor. 16:20; cf. Acts 9:30; 15:40; 2 Cor. 11:9). The plural 'brothers' is also used in commands or statements concerning Christians in general (Heb. 2:11,12,17; 1 Jn. 3:14; Rev. 12:10).

Most often, however, the term 'brothers' is used in direct address, by a speaker to his listeners, or by an author to his readers. Thus Peter refers to the disciples in the upper room (Acts 1:16), to the crowds on the day of Pentecost (Acts 2:29), to the Jerusalem council (Acts 15:7), and to the churches to whom he wrote (2 Pet. 1:10). The twelve address their fellow-believers as 'brothers' in Acts 6:3; Stephen uses the same term with the Sanhedrin in Acts 7:2, as also does Paul in Acts 23:1,5,6. Paul addresses his readers as 'brothers' numerous times in his letters to the Romans, Corinthians, Galatians, Ephesians, and Thessalonians; so also do James and the author of Hebrews.

It is interesting to note that whenever 'brother' or 'brothers' is used in direct address, it is to a fellow-Jew (whether believing or non-believing) or to a fellow-Christian.[3] Among Jews, of course, the term is appropriate because of their shared physical descent through Abraham, Isaac, and Jacob. Among Christians, however, whether Jew or Gentile, the word 'brother' attests to the new

---

[3] Note that when Paul speaks to the hostile Jewish crowd in Jerusalem he nevertheless calls them 'brothers' (Acts 22:1); but when he addresses a predominantly Gentile group of non-believers aboard ship, he calls them simply 'men (*andres*)' (Acts 27:10,21,25).

spiritual family connection formed through common faith in Jesus Christ.

In the New Testament world, the brother/sister relationship was especially close. This point should be kept in mind when reading exhortations such as Paul's command to Timothy to treat 'younger women as sisters, with absolute purity' (1 Tim. 5:2), or the instruction to greet one another with a holy kiss (Rom. 16:16; 1 Cor. 16:20; 2 Cor. 13:12; 1 Thess. 5:26; 1 Pet. 5:14).

BUILDER, EXPERT

In 1 Corinthians 3:10, Paul compares himself to an 'expert builder' (*architekton*), who laid the foundation at Corinth upon which others were building. In secular Greek, *tekton* meant a craftsman or builder who worked with wood, stone, or metal, and the *architekton* referred to the master craftsman or head builder who supervised the others.

Earlier in 1 Corinthians 3, Paul has explained that some leadership roles precede others; just as one plants and another waters, some begin the work that others continue. The 'expert builder' is one of those initiating and founding leadership roles. Yet, says Paul, even the contribution of the expert builder has no permanence unless it is used to establish a work on the foundation of Jesus Christ himself (3:11). The 'expert builder' is not a totally independent agent; rather his ministry, like every other, comes about as a response to the prior call of God, and must be conducted according to God's design. Paul further acknowledges that he laid the foundation 'by the grace God has given me' (3:10). Just as the ministry of leadership originates in the grace of God, it also depends on the grace of God for its execution.

BUILDING (see also FOUNDATION, PILLAR, TEMPLE)

Some of the most important and frequently used metaphors are those which describe how the individual believers are linked together and formed by God into an interdependent and unified whole. In Ephesians 2, a passage rich in images, Paul shifts in verse 20 from the metaphors of citizenship and membership in a household to the image of a building. He describes the apostles and the prophets as the foundation, Jesus Christ as the cornerstone, and then individual Christians as the building materials. In verse 21 he says that in Christ 'the whole building (*oikodome*) is joined together and rises to become a holy temple in the Lord'. Then in verse 22 he says that 'you too are being built together to become a dwelling in which God lives by his Spirit'.

In 1 Corinthians 3, another passage where a number of metaphors mix together, Paul says, 'You are God's field, God's building' (v. 9). Then he describes himself as the master builder who laid the foundation for the building.

The metaphor of the building speaks not only of the believers' special relationship to God – as his dwelling place, as those who belong to him, and as those who are built upon Jesus the cornerstone and foundation – but also of their relationship to one another. They have been fitted together with the same skill employed by a stonemason, each stone carefully placed in relation to the ones around it, each one doing its part to hold up the entire structure, together fulfilling the purpose of providing a dwelling place for the Holy Spirit.

C

CHILD

Since there are several Greek words translated as 'child' in various New Testament contexts, we will examine each of them in this section. First we will consider the word *hyios*, which literally means 'son', but which can also be used in a more generic sense for 'child'.

Jesus' first usage of the 'child' metaphor to describe his disciples occurs in the Beatitudes, where he promises, 'Blessed are the peacemakers, for they will be called sons (*hyioi*) of God' (Mt. 5:9). The children of God are those who share his character, in whom can be seen the family resemblance. Later in the Sermon on the Mount Jesus exhorts his disciples to love their enemies and to pray for their persecutors so that 'you may be sons of your Father in heaven' (Mt. 5:45). The remainder of that paragraph builds to the climax in verse 48: 'Be perfect, therefore, as your heavenly Father is perfect.' Once again, then, to be a child of the Father is to imitate the Father's character. In a similar passage in Luke 6:35,36, Jesus summons his disciples to be 'sons of the Most High' by being merciful as their Father is merciful.

In reply to the question about the woman with multiple husbands, Jesus refers to those who will enter the age to come as 'children (*hyioi*) of God' and 'children (*hyioi*) of the resurrection' (Lk. 20:36). Then in Matthew 13:38, in the explanation of the parable of the weeds, Jesus says that the good seed are the 'sons (*hyioi*) of the kingdom'. The children of the King are the children of God.

The above are direct references to the disciples as children of God. But there are also numerous passages in which Jesus, speaking to his disciples, implies the same relationship by referring to God as '*your* Father' (emphasis mine; Mt. 5:16,45,48; 6:1,4,6,8,14,15,18,26,32; 7:11; 10:20,29; 13:43; 18:14; 23:9; Mk. 11:25; Lk. 6:36; 11:13; 12:30,32; Jn. 20:17). Notice that the great majority of these references are found in Matthew and, in particular, in the Sermon on the Mount. Furthermore, in teaching the disciples to pray, Jesus encourages them to address God as 'our Father' (Mt. 6:9; Lk. 11:2). Of course, there are also numerous verses in which Jesus refers to God as '*the* Father' (e.g. Mt. 28:19; Mk. 13:32; Jn. 4:23) or as '*my* Father' (e.g. Mt. 26:39; Lk. 22:29; Jn. 10:29), especially in the gospel of John. But here we are focusing on the passages which reveal Jesus' emphasis on the specific, personal relationship between the disciples and their heavenly Father.

These passages repeatedly associate two things with the image of the disciples as children of the Father: first, the family resemblance, or the similarity in character between the Father and the children; and second, the tender care that the Father shows toward his children, listening to their prayers, providing for their needs, and rewarding them for their faithful service.

In Luke 10:21–23, following the return of the 72 from their mission, Jesus praises God because he has 'hidden these things from the wise and learned, and revealed them to little children (*nepiois*)' (10:21; parallel to Mt. 11:25–27). Jesus says that the only ones who really know the Father are the Son and those to whom the Son reveals the Father. God has hidden these things from some and revealed them to others. The phrase 'little children' here translates a single word, *nepios*. Here Jesus' use of the image of the little child to describe his disciples underscores their ignorance apart from divine revelation. Whatever they understand is by the gracious action of God.

On several occasions Jesus uses a child as an illustration of the sort of qualities that should characterize his followers. For example, in Matthew 18:1, his disciples ask him, 'Who is the greatest in the kingdom of heaven?' The parallel passages in Mark 9:33–37 and Luke 9:46–48 reveal that the question arose out of an argument among the disciples about which of them in particular *was* the greatest. Jesus replies by calling over a little child, and saying, 'Whoever humbles himself like this child (*paidion*) is the greatest in the kingdom of heaven' (Mt. 18:4). Here we find yet a third word translated 'child' (*paidion*). Using the strongest possible negative expression, Jesus says, 'Unless you change and become like little children, you *will never* enter the kingdom of heaven' (18:3; emphasis mine). He goes on to speak of the importance of welcoming even a child (18:5), and of the seriousness of causing one of the little ones who believe in him to sin (18:6). He warns against the temptation to look down on these little ones (18:10), reminding the disciples of the guardian angels who are watching (18:11). He affirms that the heavenly Father does not want one of them to be lost (18:14). When Jesus speaks of 'little ones' in these verses, he is probably continuing the reference to the child, who is standing there in the midst.

Jesus was issuing a warning, a rebuke of the attitude that led to the question about greatness in the first place. The disciples were inclined to shoo the children away (cf. Mt. 19:13–15, with parallels to Mk. 10:13–16 and Lk. 18:15–17). But the person who did not consider a child to be very important, said Jesus, showed a fundamental lack of humility, and therefore was unfit to enter the kingdom of heaven. These warnings were issued not to unbelievers, or to the undecided, but to those who were already following Jesus. The humility of a child, illustrated in a welcoming attitude toward the child, was an essential mark of true discipleship.

Jesus also uses the child as an illustration of the sincere and simple faith which is required of the disciple. In Luke 18:17, when parents bring babies to Jesus to have him touch them, Jesus states bluntly, 'Anyone who will not receive the kingdom of God like a little child (*paidion*) will never enter it.'

On one occasion, Jesus addresses the disciples affectionately as 'children'. In John 21, after the resurrection, when he sees six of the disciples fishing on the Sea of Galilee early in the morning, Jesus calls out to them, 'Friends (*paidia*), haven't you any fish?' (John 21:5). Here it seems to be a term of endearing address, somewhat as one might use the term 'boys' to talk to male comrades in English.

Two other terms for children appear on the lips of Jesus: 'child' (*teknon*, which has no reference to particular age or gender) and 'little child' (*teknion*). After the departure of Judas from the upper room, Jesus addresses the disciples with this endearing term: 'My children (*teknia*), I will be with you only a little longer' (Jn. 13:33). Jesus uses this tender expression in telling the disciples that he must soon leave them. He knows that this revelation will arouse some fear and uncertainty among them, so he addresses them gently, like a parent with young children.

In Matthew 9:2 (and in the parallel passage in Mk. 2:5), Jesus speaks to the paralysed man who has been let down through the roof by his friends: 'Take heart, son (*teknon*); your sins are forgiven.' Jesus uses this term at the very outset of the encounter, communicating warmth and acceptance to a person who may have been feeling quite conspicuous, uncertain, and ill at ease under the circumstances.

Mark 10:24 records one other incident where Jesus addresses his disciples as 'children'. After the disciples react with amazement to Jesus' statement about the difficulty of a rich man being saved, Jesus says, 'Children (*tekna*), how hard it is to enter the kingdom of God!' Again, the use of this term communicates love and reassurance in a situation of uncertainty.

Each of the terms for 'child' that Jesus used for his disciples – *hyios*, *nepios*, *paidion*, *teknos*, and *teknion* – are taken up by other New Testament writers as well. Just as Jesus used the image of 'child (*hyios*) of God' to teach that his followers should imitate the character of their heavenly Father, so Paul invokes the same metaphor in teaching the Corinthians about their need to live a life of separation from the world (2 Cor. 6:18).[1] Jesus also used the 'son (*hyios*)'

---

[1] In this quotation Paul combines and modifies several Old Testament passages, taking God's promise to make us his children, and making explicit the reference to daughters as well as sons: 'you will be my sons and daughters'; this is the only example of the figurative use of the term 'daughter' for a Christian believer in the New Testament letters. But Jesus used this word to address the woman with the issue of blood: 'Daughter (*thygater*), your faith has healed you' (Mk. 5:34; cf. Mt. 9:22).

image to teach about the tender care of God for his children; in this same spirit the author of Hebrews assures his readers that God's disciplinary actions are proof that 'God is treating you as sons (*hyiois*)' (12:7), an expression of his love.

Paul uses the 'child' (*hyios*) terminology in Romans and Galatians to describe the Christian's deliverance from bondage and fear (Rom. 8:14,19; Gal. 3:7,26; 4:7). The Christian is no longer a slave, or a prisoner, or under the supervision of a tutor. Sonship is an image of maturity and freedom, of privilege and elevation of status. In the same way, the author of Hebrews celebrates Christ's action in 'bringing many sons to glory' (2:10), and John records God's announcement in the vision of the new heavens and new earth: 'He who overcomes will inherit all this, and I will be his God and he will be my son' (Rev. 21:7).

In each of these references to 'child/son' (*hyios*), every Christian is seen as a child of God. However, this word can also be used in a narrower sense, by a senior leader referring to a younger believer. Peter conveys greetings from 'my son Mark' (1 Pet. 5:13), expressing a depth of respect and love for this younger man.

Another word for 'child' (*teknon*) is similarly used in two senses – to describe believers as God's children, but also to refer to younger or newer members of the fellowship as spiritual children in relation to their leaders. Only senior members of the community use the term in this second sense.

In Romans 8, Paul uses both words for 'child' (*teknon* and *hyios*) interchangeably to speak of the privileges of freedom and rights of inheritance that accompany sonship (vv. 16,17,21); similar themes accompany his use of *teknon* in Galatians 4:28,31. The apostle John likewise expresses amazement at the privilege that is ours in being called God's children (1 Jn. 3:1,2). In several other passages, believers are reminded that they are God's children, responsible to display the family resemblance as part of the call to holy living (Eph. 5:1,2; Phil. 2:15; 1 Pet. 1:14–17; 1 Jn. 3:10; 5:2).

Drawing from the technical legal vocabulary of his day, Paul introduces a term closely related to 'son/child' (*hyios*) that refers to both the process and the state of adoption (*hyiothesia*). In Romans 9:4, Paul uses this term for God's adoption of the nation of Israel, but in the following four passages, it refers to God's gracious act of making us his children:

> You did not receive a spirit that makes you a slave again to fear, but you received the Spirit of *sonship* (Rom. 8:15);
>
> We wait eagerly for our *adoption as sons*, the redemption of our bodies (Rom. 8:23);
>
> But when the time had fully come, God sent his Son, born of a woman, born under law, to redeem those under law, that we might receive the *full rights of sons* (Gal. 4:4,5);
>
> In love he predestined us to be *adopted as his sons* through Jesus Christ (Eph. 1:4,5).

In these passages we see that adoption implies freedom from fear, intimacy with God, hope for the future, release from bondage to the law, and experience of the gracious love of God. The concept of adoption emphasizes that the relationship of sonship is an honour, a privilege, a blessing, something that we have no right to expect or to demand.

On several occasions Paul appeals to those whom he has nurtured or led to the Lord, calling them his son or his children (*teknos*, singular, or *tekna*, plural):

> I am not writing this to shame you, but to warn you, as my dear children (1 Cor. 4:14);
> I am sending to you Timothy, my son whom I love (1 Cor. 4:17);
> I speak as to my children – open wide your hearts also (2 Cor. 6:13);
> My dear children, for whom I am again in the pains of childbirth until Christ is formed in you (Gal. 4:19);
> To Titus, my true son in our common faith (Tit. 1:4);
> I appeal to you for my son Onesimus (Philem. 10).

In each of these passages we can hear the strong tone of Paul's affection and intense concern, combined with a sense of responsibility for the welfare of his spiritual children.

Several times in his first letter, the apostle John refers to his readers as 'dear children (*teknia*)', a nursery term that denotes a little child rather than offspring in general. It is not surprising that the 'apostle of love', probably well along in years at the time of writing, would use such a tender expression for his spiritual family.

The word for 'infant' (*nepios*) implies helplessness and inexperience. As we have seen, Jesus uses the term in Luke 10:21–23 to contrast the 'wise' of this world, who remain ignorant of God's truth, with the 'little children' to whom the things of the Spirit have been revealed. In each of the three places where this metaphor is taken up by the New Testament authors, it is used to describe believers as they are, but not as they should be. Paul scolds the Corinthians for being 'mere infants in Christ' (1 Cor. 3:1), still needing milk and not ready for solid food, because of their jealous rivalries and fixation on human personalities. In Ephesians 4:14–16 Paul looks forward to the day when, after the equipping gifts have produced unity and maturity, 'we will no longer be infants,' troubled by doctrinal instability. Similarly the author of Hebrews contrasts the infant, still living on milk, with the mature person who has learned to distinguish good from evil (Heb. 5:13). In each of these instances the metaphor is used with a tone of rebuke. Everybody starts as an infant, but nobody needs to remain as an infant.

The remaining word for 'child' used by Jesus in reference to his followers is *paidion*. The author of Hebrews also employs this term in describing Jesus' identification with us: 'Since the children have flesh and blood, he too shared in their humanity' (2:14). John twice addresses the recipients of his first letter as 'children (*paidia*)' (2:13,18).

CHOSEN

Although many of the terms Jesus uses for his disciples convey very vivid pictures, the idea of the 'chosen' is less concrete. Because of the long history of the reference to Israel as God's chosen people (Deut. 10:15; Isa. 41:8), Jesus' reference to his followers as chosen ones (*eklektoi*), or the 'elect', evokes images of them as the new Israel, the true remnant. It is a term which emphasizes the privileges which believers enjoy as objects of God's gracious choice.

Jesus uses the related verb, 'to choose' (*eklegomai*), several times in the gospel of John in reference to his disciples: 'Have I not chosen you, the Twelve?' (6:70); 'I know those I have chosen' (13:18); 'You did not choose me, but I chose you' (15:16); 'I have chosen you out of the world' (15:19).

Elsewhere, Jesus uses the noun on two occasions. The first instance is Luke 18, in the parable of the persistent widow. Having described how the reluctant judge finally gives in to the widow's pleas, Jesus draws the application: 'Will not God bring about justice for his chosen ones, who cry out to him day and night?' (18:7). Jesus' use of the term 'chosen' expresses a guarantee of protection and preservation for those who must endure hardship and persecution. Those whom God has selected and embraced in his love will never be abandoned to their enemies.

The same theme of protection in the midst of adversity is expressed through Jesus' use of the term during his discourse on the Mount of Olives, recorded in Matthew 24 and Mark 13. In response to the disciples' questions about the end of the age, Jesus describes a time of increasing stress and persecution. But then he adds the word of hope: 'If those days had not been cut short, no-one would survive, but for the sake of the elect (*eklektous*) those days will be shortened' (Mt. 24:22). Mark records the same statement, with an additional modifying phrase (emphasis mine): '. . . the elect, *whom he has chosen*' (Mk. 13:20).

Jesus warns that false prophets and false Messiahs will appear so convincing that even the elect would be deceived, 'if it were possible' (Mt. 24:24; Mk. 13:22). That qualifying phrase, recorded by both evangelists, implies a promise that those whom God has chosen will nevertheless be preserved from final deception. Then comes another promise – the sending of God's angels to 'gather his elect from the four winds, from the ends of the earth to the ends of the heavens' (Mk. 13:27; cf. Mt. 24:31).

The inclusion of the personal pronoun 'his', in reference to the elect, emphasizes the bond between God and his people.

Once again, as in Luke 18, we see this metaphor introduced as part of a comforting promise, that God will come to the rescue of his people before the time of suffering overwhelms them completely. He has committed himself to protect and preserve those who are his, those whom he has chosen.

Paul uses the term in the same way in Romans 8:33, when he asks, 'Who will bring any charge against those whom God has chosen (*eklekton*)?' God is the defender of those whom he has gathered by his grace. The fact that believers are chosen by God is their guarantee of security, in spite of their weakness or their sinfulness, both now and in the life to come.

In Romans 16:13, Paul sends his greetings to Rufus, addressing him as 'chosen in the Lord', a phrase which could have been applied to any Christian. In his pastoral letters Paul uses the term 'chosen' or 'elect' in reference to believers in general. In 2 Timothy 2:10 he says, 'I endure everything for the sake of the elect', and in Titus 1:1 he identifies himself as an apostle of Jesus Christ 'for the faith of God's elect'. For Paul, to see people as 'chosen by God' is no excuse for personal inaction. Rather, he sees himself as the means by which God's choice is realized. He gladly expends himself for the sake of those on whom God has placed such high value.

To be chosen by God is to enjoy a great honour. Yet to be chosen by God is not only to enjoy privilege, but also to assume a responsibility. Peter addresses his first letter to 'God's elect . . . we have been chosen according to the foreknowledge of God the Father . . . for obedience to Jesus

Christ and sprinkling by his blood' (1 Pet. 1:1,2). In bringing together the idea of God's choice with the responsibility for obedience, Peter reminds his readers of the purpose of their selection. The same ethical dimension appears in Paul's exhortation to the Colossians, where he urges them 'as God's chosen people, holy and dearly loved' to live lives of compassion, kindness, humility, gentleness, patience, forgiveness, love, peace, and thankfulness (Col. 3:12–17).

CHRISTIAN

The term 'Christian' (*Christianos*) did not arise from within the Christian community, but as a somewhat mocking nickname employed by outsiders. Nevertheless, it was soon adopted by the early disciples as a badge of identification with their Lord. As first used in Antioch (Acts 11:26), the nickname expressed the fact that the disciples were seen as followers of the 'Christ-sect', much like those loyal to Herod were called the 'Herodians' (Mk. 3:6; 12:13; Mt. 22:16). Perhaps the term also indicated that, for better or for worse, depending on the perspective of the observer, these people were speaking and behaving much like Christ.

In Acts 26:28, in a tone of mild sarcasm, Agrippa asks Paul, 'Do you think that in such a short time you can persuade me to be a Christian?' In his first letter, Peter encourages his readers: 'If you suffer as a Christian, do not be ashamed, but praise God that you bear that name' (1 Pet. 4:16). In both cases, the term is introduced in contexts where believers are being scorned or persecuted for their identification with Jesus Christ.

CHURCH

Sometimes terms become so familiar that we forget the imagery that originally lay behind them. Such may be the case with the word normally translated 'church' (*ekklesia*). It is one of the terms used most frequently to describe the community of followers of Jesus, although it occurs only once on the lips of Jesus, in the well-known statement to Peter in Matthew 16:18: 'And I tell you that you are Peter, and on this rock I will build my church, and the gates of Hades will not overcome it.'

The word 'church' is used in several senses. In the first place, it commonly refers to the gathering of Christians in a particular locality. Thus we find references to particular cities – the church at Jerusalem (Acts 8:1), at Antioch (13:1), in Cenchrea (Rom. 16:1), and in Corinth (1 Cor. 1:2; 2 Cor. 1:1), as well as the church of the Laodiceans (Col. 4:15), and of the Thessalonians (1 Thess. 1:1). There are specific references to the church in Priscilla and Aquila's house (Rom. 16:4,5; 1 Cor. 16:19), and in Nympha's house (Col. 4:15), in addition to general geographic references to the church throughout Judea, Galilee, and Samaria (Acts 9:31), the churches throughout Syria and Cilicia (Acts 15:41), the Galatian churches (1 Cor. 16:1), the churches in the province of Asia (1 Cor. 16:19), the Macedonian churches (2 Cor. 8:1), and the churches of Judea (Gal. 1:22).

In many other passages, 'church' refers to a group (or groups) of Christians meeting together regularly in the same locality, even if the specific geographic reference is not stated, as in the following examples:

. . . what I teach everywhere in every church (1 Cor. 4:17);

> . . . when you come together as a church (1 Cor. 11:18);
> Show these men the proof of your love and the reason
>   for our pride in you, so that the churches can see it
>   (2 Cor. 8:24);
> . . . not one church shared with me in respect to giving
>   and receiving, except you only (Phil. 4:15);
> He should call the elders of the church to pray over him
>   (Jas. 5:14);
> They have told the church about your love (3 John 6).

Some passages use 'church' in a more universal sense, to denote Christians in general, but still at a particular time and in identifiable places, as when Paul says, 'I persecuted the church of God' (1 Cor. 15:9; Gal. 1:13). But there is an even broader and loftier usage of the term 'church', in passages like Ephesians 1:22, which states that Christ has been appointed 'head over everything for the church', and Ephesians 5:23–32, in which Paul compares the love of a husband for his wife to that of Christ for the church. In one of the most magnificent tributes to Christ in all of Scripture, Paul says that Christ is 'the head of the body, the church' (Col. 1:18). The author of Hebrews says that his readers have come 'to the church of the first-born, whose names are written in heaven' (12:23).

Thus 'church' (*ekklesia*) has a broad range of references, from a specific group of Christians gathered in a home, to all of the assemblies in a given geographical area, to the entire group of believers in Christ, past and present, on earth and in heaven, seen as a whole. But certain aspects of the term can be seen through all the usages.

In the first place, it is clear that 'church' refers to *people*, not to buildings or to institutional structures. In New Testament usage, churches can decide, welcome, gather, pray, send greetings, enjoy peace, be grateful, enjoy hospitality, praise, choose, see, share, and suffer. They can also be destroyed, seized by fear, stumble, be despised, edified, persecuted, burdened, and imitated. These are all words that describe people, not bricks or organizational charts.

The use of such verbs in connection with 'church' also indicates that the church is a group of people connected together, acting in harmony, sharing feelings and experiences – and not merely an abstraction or a theoretical way of grouping people, like saying 'all left-handed people' or 'those with March birthdays'. The church is comprised of people vitally interrelated with one another, because Christ has called them together.

Originally *ekklesia* ('church') was a military word, referring to a call for the army to assemble. Later it came to be used of a civic gathering, referring to a group of people called together. Thus 'church' describes a group of people brought together not by their own initiative, but by God's, not by their voluntary decision to associate, but by their response to the prior call of God. And it describes those who enjoy the full rights and privileges of the community; there are no second-class citizens or outsiders in the church; all have the rights of citizens, all are under the covenant.

Closely related to the term 'church' (*ekklesia*), or the community of those who have been called together, is the word 'called' (*kletos*). Whereas the first word focuses on the assembly of the group in response to the call, the second word emphasizes the personal summons itself. 'Called' is passive. The actor is God. We are seen not as initiators but as responders, as those moving forward because of the summons.

A number of passages speak of Christians in general as being 'called'. Thus Paul addresses the Romans as those 'called to belong to Jesus Christ' (1:6) and 'called to be saints' (1:7; cf. 1 Cor. 1:2). In Romans 8:28 he affirms that 'in all things God works for the good of those who love him, who have been called according to his purpose'; the following verses spell out the purpose of that call: to be justified, glorified, and conformed to the image of God's Son. Thus the calling is not to a specific vocation, but to a pattern of holy living. Paul also refers to the Corinthians as 'those whom God has called' (1 Cor. 1:24), and in the first verse of his letter, Jude addresses 'those who have been called', without further qualification or elaboration.

On two occasions Paul speaks of being called in a more specific sense. In Romans 1:1 he identifies himself as 'called to be an apostle'. In 1 Corinthians 1:1 he expands the same phrase to 'called to be an apostle of Christ Jesus by the will of God'. The addition of the reference to God's will further emphasizes that his ministry is a response to God's summons. The call comes from outside and above; his ministry is neither a self-chosen vocation nor the expression of an inner urge to find his destiny.

CITIZEN

Three images introduced in the New Testament letters are drawn from the institution of the Greek city-state. The Greeks considered the city-state (*polis*) to be the best possible structure in which people could associate. Under Roman rule these city-states still continued to enjoy a considerable degree of freedom, as long as they did not antagonize the Roman authorities. The privileges of democracy in these city-states were available only to citizens. Foreigners and slaves were explicitly excluded.

In some cases, the early Christians could claim the privilege of citizenship (as, for example, Paul did to great advantage more than once, e.g. Acts 16:37; 22:25; 25:11). But in many more cases, Christians had no such social advantage. Thus, to be described as citizens of a *heavenly* city brought great security and comfort.

The author of Hebrews speaks of the city (*polis*) to which Abraham and the other patriarchs looked forward, the place that lay at the end of their pilgrimage (11:10,16). These sojourners became symbols for Christians, who also looked forward to a future place of belonging with God. The heavenly Jerusalem has both a present and a future aspect, representing the whole people of God, past and present, on earth and in heaven. Thus the author of Hebrews says: 'You have come to Mount Zion, to the heavenly Jerusalem, the city of the living God' (12:22). The future aspect of the city comes to the foreground once again in the next chapter: 'For here we do not have an enduring city, but we are looking for the city that is to come' (13:14). The church is a future-oriented community. Its real identity and significance will be revealed in the age to come. Its best days lie ahead.

Another metaphor related to the Greek city-state occurs once in Philippians 3:20, where Paul says: 'Our citizenship (*politeuma*) is in heaven.' Paul has been talking about straining toward the goal of God's heavenward call and has been expressing sorrow over those whose minds are earth-bound, and who can think only of their stomachs. In the verses that follow he speaks of waiting for a Saviour from heaven who will transform our bodies. The citizenship metaphor thus pulls God's people upward and forward, inspiring them to live holy lives in the present.

One other citizenship metaphor emphasizes not so much the connection with heaven, but the interrelationship with fellow-citizens. In Ephesians Paul describes how Jesus Christ has torn down the barriers that used to separate Jews from Gentiles. He says to the Gentiles: 'You are no longer foreigners and aliens, but fellow-citizens (*sympolitai*) with God's people and members of God's household' (Eph. 2:19).

CREATION, NEW

Paul says in 2 Corinthians 5:17: 'If anyone is in Christ, he is a new creation (*kaine ktisis*)'. Paul's omission of a second verb ('he is') in the Greek sentence makes the phrase 'new creation' stand out even more dramatically – thus, 'If anyone is in Christ: *new creation!*' Paul seems to recall God's work of creation in Genesis 1, where God spoke, and it came to be. Creation is something that only God can do. The only source for the Christian's new life is God himself.

In Galatians 6:15 Paul says to the Galatians, who were so obsessed with human effort and activity as the path to holiness and acceptance with God: 'Neither circumcision nor uncircumcision means anything, what counts is a new creation.' The only righteousness which God accepts is that which he himself creates. The person who has thus been made new by God has a higher status than any human achievement or nobility of birth can possibly confer.

CROWN

Twice Paul refers to believers as his crown (*stephanos*). He tells the Philippians that he loves them and longs for them, that they are his 'joy and crown' (4:1). To the Thessalonians he writes: 'What is our hope, our joy, or the crown in which we will glory in the presence of our Lord Jesus Christ when he comes? Is it not you?' (1 Thess. 2:19).

Usually 'crown' throughout the Greek world referred to the wreath of leaves bestowed to victors in athletic events. The state also awarded wreaths worked in gold as a mark of high honour. The 'crown' was thus associated with victory, celebration, worship, royalty, and public honour. When Paul calls these two churches, with whom he has such affectionate relationships, his 'crown', he is using a symbol of accomplishment, of victory won, of mission fulfilled. The establishment of a healthy church validates the ministry of the church-planter. The 'crown' metaphor also implies that a struggle has been won, that the goal has been achieved in spite of opposition and obstacles.

D

DISCIPLE

Numerous times the gospel writers speak of the followers of Jesus as his 'disciples'. In fact, this is the term most commonly used to refer to those who responded to Jesus' call. But Jesus himself also often applied the term 'disciples' to his followers. For example, in Matthew 10:42, he says, 'If anyone gives a cup of cold water to one of these little ones because he is my disciple, I tell you the truth, he will certainly not lose his reward.'

The basic meaning of 'disciple' (*mathetes*) is 'learner'. In Greek usage someone was called a 'disciple' when he apprenticed himself to someone in order to gain knowledge and practical skills. Ordinarily 'disciples' volunteered to join their teacher's 'school'; but Jesus issued a decisive call (and sometimes even discouraged those who tried to volunteer). Furthermore, disciples in the other schools expected to graduate and to become 'masters' themselves, but Jesus called people to a lifelong surrender and commitment to follow.

The word 'disciple' (*mathetes*) is often paired with 'teacher' (*didaskalos*). For example, when Jesus sends his disciples ahead to arrange for the Passover meal, he instructs them to say to a certain man, 'The Teacher says: My appointed time is near. I am going to celebrate the Passover with my disciples at your house' (Mt. 26:18; cf. Mk. 14:14; Lk. 22:11). Or again, in Matthew 10:24 and Luke 6:40 Jesus says, 'A student (*mathetes*) is not above his teacher'. In the Matthew passage, the application is that the disciple can be expected to experience the same sort of persecution suffered by his teacher; in Luke, the saying is set in the context of warnings against hypocrisy, and is used to make the point that the goal of the disciple's training is ultimately to be like his teacher. Jesus says, 'Everyone who is fully trained will be like his teacher' (Lk. 6:40). Thus to be a disciple is not to be a mere listener in a classroom; rather it is to learn a pattern of life, to adopt the lifestyle of the teacher. Although the disciple is under the authority of the teacher, it is a relationship which the student enters voluntarily, born out of his desire to become like the teacher.

In four passages Jesus defines the qualifications for those who want to be known as his disciples. In Luke 14, we read that large crowds were following Jesus. Apparently many were getting caught up with his popularity, swept along in the adventure without reflecting deeply on what they were doing. So Jesus speaks to them about the cost of discipleship. In verse 26 he lists virtually every primary relationship of kinship – father, mother, wife, children, brothers, and sisters. And he says that the one who comes to him must hate all these, and even his own life. Apart from this radical commitment, expressed through the hyperbolic reference to hatred, one cannot be Jesus' disciple. Thus it is not enough simply to come to Jesus – one must also surrender unconditionally to him.

In verse 27 of Luke 14 Jesus says further that one cannot be his disciple unless he carries his own cross and comes after Jesus. There is a difference between coming *to* Jesus and coming *after* Jesus. The first is merely encounter; the second is active obedience.

Discipleship, says Jesus, involves not only surrender of family ties, and giving up the right to self-preservation, but also requires a willingness to part with every material possession. He warns, 'Any of you who does not give up everything he has cannot be my disciple' (Lk. 14:33). Discipleship, therefore, is a radical commitment, a bond which looses all other bonds, a direction which gives life one and only one central point of reference. To be a disciple is to turn from, and to turn to. It is to sever the old loyalties and to follow after Jesus, not distracted by ties to possessions or family or even by instincts of self-protection.

Three more definitions of discipleship are given by Jesus in the gospel of John. In John chapter 8, Jesus addressed 'the Jews who had believed him' (8:31); but as the subsequent conversation demonstrated, their belief was quite superficial. So Jesus raised the issue of true discipleship. Were these people indeed the devoted followers that they seemed to be? He said, 'If you hold to my teaching, you are really my disciples' (8:31). Thus Jesus implied that there are those who followed, who associated with Jesus, but who were not really *learning* from him as their teacher; they were not reorienting their worldview or adjusting their behaviour in light of his revealed truth.

In John 8:32, Jesus states one of the benefits enjoyed by the person who holds to his teaching: 'Then you will know the truth, and the truth will set you free.' In verses 34 through 36 Jesus explains the sort of freedom he has in mind

– freedom from the compulsion to commit sin. So then, the teaching of Jesus changes life at the behavioural and ethical level. To be a disciple means not only to receive an infusion of knowledge but also to undergo a transformation of character.

Jesus' next statement about discipleship is found in his introduction of the 'new commandment' in John 13. After urging the disciples to love one another just as he has loved them, he says, 'All men will know that you are my disciples if you love one another' (13:35). The command to love is not new in itself (cf. Lev. 19:18) – but the measure of that love is new. The standard is now the self-sacrificing love that led Jesus to wash the feet of the disciples, and which would soon lead him to death on the cross for their redemption. The disciples are to display this love so consistently and openly that even people outside the community of faith will recognize that such love can only be explained by its source in the disciple's relationship to Jesus.

Jesus' final statement on the evidence for true discipleship is found in John 15:8. He has been teaching about the vine and the branches, and the focus has been on the goal of fruit-bearing. Branches that bear fruit are pruned so that they will produce even more (15:2). Only those branches that remain in the vine are capable of bearing fruit (15:4,5). God is glorified when much fruit is borne (15:8). But more than that, abundant fruitfulness is the mark of true discipleship: 'This is to my Father's glory, that you bear much fruit, showing yourselves to be my disciples' (15:8). It is the visible products of the life, the good deeds that glorify the Father and the beneficial impact upon others, enlisting them as followers of Jesus, that prove the genuineness of discipleship.

So then, when in Matthew 28:18–20 Jesus sent the disciples out with the command, 'Go and make disciples (*matheteusate*) of all nations', there was a context which the disciples would have understood. In the first place, Jesus had enlisted *them* as his disciples. Now he was exhorting them to go and do the same, to lead others into the same process of deepening relationship and ministry development into which he had conducted them. In the second place, Jesus had defined the characteristics of a true disciple – in terms of unqualified commitment, faithfulness to his word, love for fellow-disciples, and abundant fruit-bearing. The mission of the disciples was now to go out into the world to enlist and to develop *that* sort of person – to 'make disciples'!

The mission had two aspects. First, they were to baptize the disciples in the name of the Father and of the Son and of the Holy Spirit, that is, to call them to repentance and to public identification with the community of the Messiah. Second, they were to teach them to observe all things that Jesus had commanded. Note that the emphasis was not on teaching them all things, but on teaching them *to obey*. Again we see that the emphasis in discipleship is not merely on the cognitive but also on the behavioural.

Jesus assures the disciples of an ongoing relationship with them: 'Surely I will be with you always, to the very end of the age.' The disciples will *remain* disciples of the Master. They will never 'graduate' from the school of discipleship, or cease to be disciples. But they have the task of inviting others to join them as disciples of the one Master (cf. Mt. 23:8–10). They are not called to enlist disciples of *themselves*, but rather disciples of *Jesus*.

Outside of the four gospels, all of the occurrences of the word 'disciple' are found in the book of Acts, beginning in chapter 6 and continuing through chapter 21. Never is the word used in the restricted sense for the twelve (as it is sometimes in the gospels). Rather, it is Luke's general term for Christians, used in the same way as 'believer' or 'brother'. The identification of 'disciple' with 'Christian' is made explicit in Acts 11:26, where we read: 'The disciples were first called Christians at Antioch.'

Usually 'disciples' occurs in the plural, but a few individuals are also called 'disciple' in Acts: Ananias (9:10), Saul (9:26), Tabitha (9:36), Timothy (16:2), and Mnason (21:16). The term is used for both new and established believers, and for both Jews and Gentiles. In general it refers to the rank and file of believers. Nowhere is a church leader or apostle explicitly called a 'disciple'. The verb 'to make disciples' (*matheteuo*; cf. Mt. 28:19) occurs in Acts 14:21, where we read that in Lystra and Derbe Paul and Barnabas 'won a large number of disciples (*matheteusantes*)'. This passage, besides illustrating that the apostles' activities were in obedience to Jesus' great commission, indicates that believers could be called 'disciples' from the very onset of conversion. In addition to Luke's own use of the term as narrator in Acts, 'disciples' is also found in Peter's remarks to the Jerusalem Council in Acts 15:10, where he asks, 'Why do you try to test God by putting on the necks of the disciples a yoke that neither we nor our fathers have been able to bear?'

Only twice in Acts is 'disciple' associated with any leader other than the Lord. In Acts 9:25 we read that '[Saul's] followers (*mathetai*) took him by night and lowered him in a basket', thus enabling him to escape from Damascus. Notice that here the reference to these people as 'disciples' is Luke's expression, not Paul's. Then in Acts 20:30 Paul warns the Ephesian elders about false teachers who will emerge in their fellowship 'to draw away disciples after them'.

It is striking that a term used so frequently by the gospel writers, and found so often on the lips of Jesus, should be so completely unused by the leaders of the early church in reference to those that they themselves brought to the Lord and nurtured in faith – especially in view of the popularity in today's church of the vocabulary of 'discipling' and references to '*my* disciples'. Perhaps the reluctance of the New Testament writers to use this term arose because they associated it with apprenticeship to the Lord himself, not to any human leader. Thus when they heard the Lord's command to 'Go and make disciples' (Mt. 28:19), they understood the emphasis to be on persuading people to follow Jesus, rather than on gathering a group of followers around themselves.

In the book of Acts the radical commitment involved in the *mathetes* role is not made as explicit as it is in the gospels, perhaps because Luke is assuming knowledge of his first book. However, the application of the term to the entire community of believers is a reminder that for anyone to follow Jesus is to enrol in a school from which one never graduates.

E

ELDER

The term used most frequently for leaders of the New Testament congregations is 'elder' (*presbyteros*). The basic meaning of the term denotes someone who is older. Unlike most of the other terms for leadership, this one originates in well-known patterns within the Jewish community, where authority rested with heads of families. The elders in Israel were responsible for judicial, political, and military decisions. At first, all the members of the Sanhedrin were called 'elders', until later a distinction was made between lay and priestly members of the Council.

At the time of the New Testament, each synagogue had an executive committee, comprised of people who held high standing within the community. This committee attended to the secular affairs of the community. Its members were called 'elders'. The institution of 'elder' was so familiar within the Jewish community that it didn't need to be explained to the readers of the New Testament documents.

It was the elders at Jerusalem who received the gift for famine relief from the church at Antioch (Acts 11:30), and who helped to decide the basis on which Gentiles should be received into the church (Acts 15:2,4,6,22,23; 16:4). Paul and Barnabas appointed elders for each of the churches they established on their first missionary trip (Acts 14:23); later Paul instructed Titus to do the same for the churches of Crete (Tit. 1:5). Paul requested a special gathering with the elders of the church at Ephesus on his way back to Jerusalem (Acts 20:17). In his first letter to Timothy Paul gave instructions about the treatment of elders. Those who directed the affairs of the church well, especially those working at preaching and teaching, were to be given 'double honour' (5:17; in the context, a reference not only to respect, but also to reimbursement); accusations were not to be treated casually, but handled carefully with proper attention to witnesses, and willingness to give public rebuke when necessary (5:19). James called for the involvement of the elders in prayers for the sick (Jas. 5:14). Peter instructed elders about proper attitudes and motivation (1 Pet. 5:1–3), calling himself 'a fellow-elder (*sympresbuteros*)', and John the apostle referred to himself as 'the elder' in his second and third letters (2 Jn. 1; 3 Jn. 1).

As with elders in the Jewish community, the elders of the first-century church always appear as a group. References to elders in particular churches are consistently plural (e.g. Acts 14:23; 15:4; 20:17; Jas. 5:14). Thus the life of community and teamwork is expressed within the leadership of the church as well as within the life of the congregation as a whole.

EVANGELIST

An 'evangelist' (*euanggelistes*) is someone who brings good news. Although the related verb, 'to bring good news' or 'to evangelize' (*euanggelizo*), is found frequently in the New Testament, the noun occurs only three times – in the reference to Philip in Acts 21:8, in the list of equipping gifts in Ephesians 4:11, and in Paul's exhortation to Timothy to 'do the work of an evangelist' (2 Tim. 4:5). In classical Greek usage, the 'evangelist' is a messenger who brings joyful news of victory or some other welcome event.

Evangelists do not make up their own announcements. They function under the authority of the one who sent them.

EYEWITNESS (see also WITNESS)

In 2 Peter 1:16 Peter says, 'We did not follow cleverly invented stories when we told you about the power and coming of our Lord Jesus Christ, but we were eye-witnesses (*epoptai*) of his majesty.' The term 'eyewitness' derived from the verb 'to look at' (*epopeuo*). In the New Testament, when the image of the witness is used to describe followers of Jesus, it always refers to people who have personally experienced Jesus. Thus the metaphor strongly emphasizes the aspect of personal identification; it gives no room for second-hand reporting.

F

FARMER

In 2 Timothy 2:6, Paul urges Timothy to be like a 'farmer' (*georgos*) who works hard and therefore deserves a share of the crops. The reference to the 'share' implies that the farmer is working for someone else – the crops are not his to gather and store as he wills. In 1 Corinthians 3:6–8, Paul describes himself as the one who plants (*phyteuon*) and Apollos as the one who waters (*potizon*), while God is the one who causes the growth. Some workers initiate a new work; others maintain it and nurture it. But the credit for the results belongs to God alone, who assigns the different tasks to each worker. When there is growth and fruit, God is the only explanation.

FATHER / MOTHER

Jesus did not describe his disciples as 'parents' of other believers nearly as often as he described them as children. In fact, he specifically warned them against ascribing the

honorary title of 'father' to any fellow-disciple (Mt. 23:9).
In Mark 3, when he describes those who do the will of God
as his spiritual family, he refers to 'brother', 'sister', and even
'mother', but not to 'father'. Similarly, in Mark 10:29,30,
when he encourages his disciples about the benefits they
will receive in return for their sacrifices, he promises
'brothers, sisters, mothers, children', but not fathers.
Whenever Jesus uses the term 'father', he is speaking either
of literal biological descent, or of God as Father, but never
of one disciple in relation to another.

However, in the apostolic writings the metaphor of
parenthood is used fairly often, primarily by Paul. In
2 Corinthians 12:14, speaking of his readiness to sacrifice
with joy for the Corinthian believers, Paul introduces the
illustration of the parent (*goneus*) with children, saying that
'children should not have to save up for their parents, but
parents for their children'. Spiritual leaders should not be a
burden on their followers; they are called to be sacrificial
servants, expending themselves joyfully for those whom
they have helped to bring to spiritual birth, like parents with
children.

In 1 Timothy 5:1,2 Paul reminds Timothy to exhort an
older man 'as if he were your father', and to treat the 'older
women as mothers'. Thus even the spiritual leader is to
show respect for older members of the family of believers,
just as would be appropriate in the ordinary household.

In a beautifully tender passage in the first letter to the
Thessalonians, Paul describes himself and his ministry team
in maternal imagery. He says, 'We were gentle among you,
like a mother (*trophos*) caring for her little children' (1 Thess.
2:7). The word translated 'mother' here refers to a woman
nursing, whether her own children or someone else's; but
in this context, with the emphasis on love, and with the

reference to the 'father' in verse 11, it is clear that the word should be taken as 'nursing mother' rather than 'wet nurse'. The emphasis on gentleness in leadership conveyed by this image is quite striking.

The image of the spiritual leader as mother is also implied in 1 Corinthians 3:1–3, where Paul speaks of having to give them milk, not solid food, as well as in Galatians 4:19, where he speaks of the agony he has endured in the process of bringing these believers to spiritual birth: 'I am again in the pains of childbirth until Christ is formed in you.'

More often than 'mother', however, we find the image of father (*pater*). Of course, in the passages we have already seen where apostles refer to others as 'son' or 'children', the parental metaphor is implied. But several times the apostle Paul describes himself explicitly as a spiritual father. For example, Paul commends Timothy because, 'as a son with his father he has served with me in the work of the gospel' (Phil. 2:22). Note that Paul does not say, 'Timothy served me', but rather that he served 'with me'. His description of himself as father in no way implies an inferior or servile status for Timothy. In the passage from 1 Thessalonians mentioned above, Paul, Silas, and Timothy write: 'You know that we dealt with each of you as a father deals with his children, encouraging, comforting and urging you to live lives worthy of God' (1 Thess. 2:11,12). Here the emphasis of the illustration is on individualized care, on practical exhortation from the more experienced to the less experienced.

In 1 Corinthians 4:15 Paul makes his strongest assertion of spiritual fatherhood: 'Even though you have ten thousand guardians in Christ, you do not have many fathers, for in Christ Jesus I became your father through the gospel.'

Implied in this image is Paul's authority. Only a few verses later he asks, 'Shall I come to you with a whip, or in love and with a gentle spirit?' (4:21). The obvious implication is that Paul can exercise his parental powers of discipline if he has to. Yet the overall tone of the passage is that of appeal and loving persuasion, not of insistence on superior status or rights. Paul treats his spiritual children as adults. He does not attempt to keep them weak and dependent on himself.

FIELD

In 1 Corinthians 3, where Paul speaks of planting the seed at Corinth, Apollos watering it, and God causing the growth; he says, 'you are God's field (*georgion*, cultivated land)' (v. 9). The field belongs to God, and the field hands are servants assigned their tasks by him (v. 5). The field is the context for growth and development; it is full of possibilities – with proper cultivation a great harvest can be obtained. The focus of the illustration is found in the phrase in verse 6: 'God made it grow'. That is the one matter of consequence – not the names of the field hands, but the fact that God caused the crop to actually grow and flourish.

FIRSTFRUITS

An agricultural metaphor used a number of times by the New Testament writers is 'firstfruits' (*aparche*). The basic meaning of the word is the first portion, the part set aside for God before the remainder could be used. In Exodus 23 God instituted the Feast of Harvest (also called Feast of Weeks, and later, Pentecost), to be celebrated 'with the firstfruits of the crops you sow in your field' (23:16). In verse 19 God asks for the 'best of the firstfruits of your soil' – not only the first, but also the best. The offering of the firstfruits implies that there is more harvest to come; the first of the crop is given to the Lord, in full confidence that just as he has brought the crops to their initial ripeness, so he will continue his providential care until the whole harvest has been gathered.

In 1 Corinthians 16:15 Paul refers to the household of Stephanas as 'the first converts (*aparche*) in Achaia'. Their conversion was the promise of many more to come, as the Lord encouraged Paul during his initial days in Corinth: 'I have many people in this city' (Acts 18:10). Paul also extends the illustration of the firstfruits by noting that the household of Stephanas had 'devoted themselves to the service of the saints', offering themselves, as it were, on the altar, like a sacrificed offering.

James, writing to Jewish believers, said that God 'chose to give us birth through the word of truth, that we might be a kind of firstfruits of all he created' (1:18). God is here described as the creator of life, the author of new birth. In that the gospel first came to the Jews, these Jewish believers are appropriately called the 'firstfruits' of the whole community of Jews and Gentiles who together comprise the church. Furthermore, as the first generation of believers, they are the 'firstfruits' of those who will be brought to birth in years to come.

In his vision of the 144,000 in the book of Revelation, John describes them as 'offered as firstfruits to God and the Lamb' (14:4). This symbolic number has been variously interpreted. But the reference to them as 'firstfruits' should be related to the passages in Revelation about the 'multitude that no-one could count, from every nation, tribe, people and language' (7:9) who remain faithful during the great tribulation, and also relates to the proclamation of the gospel to 'every nation, tribe, language, and people' (14:6). Thus the 144,000 represent the first of a much greater number of believers to be gathered to Christ from all over the world.

The image of the firstfruits, also used of Christ as the first to rise from the dead (1 Corinthians 15:20), turns our attention toward the final harvest. It reminds us of the great worldwide mission of the church, and the task of making disciples from every nation before the Lord returns. It is an image of hope, assuring us that there are still many peoples yet to be represented around the throne of the Lamb, and that many fields are becoming ripe for harvest.

FISHERMAN

The very first metaphor which Jesus applies to his followers occurs in the familiar invitation: 'Come, follow me, and I will make you fishers (*halieis*) of men' (Mt. 4:19; Mk. 1:17). Although this has become one of the most familiar illustrations for discipleship, it is not used again by Jesus, nor is it taken up by any of the New Testament writers. Perhaps the reason why it is so prominent in our thinking is that it is the *first* image that Jesus uses to describe the life into which he is inviting his disciples.

Jesus issues his initial call to discipleship in terms of a task to be done, a mission to be accomplished. The mission focuses on the transformation of people. But the promise of effective influence in the lives of others is preceded by the command: 'Come, follow me,' or 'Come after me.' These are the words of a *leader* to a potential follower, as our English word 'leader' carries the image of one who goes ahead. Thus the invitation to the disciples as future leaders begins with the necessity of learning to be followers.

The ministry of leadership begins with the invitation of Jesus, with his call and initiative, not with volunteer enlistment. And the process of leadership development is also under his direction. Jesus says, '*I will make you* fishers of men.' That is, what the disciples become will be what Jesus makes them.

In chapter five of his gospel, Luke records the call of the first disciples, including many details that are not mentioned by either Mark or Matthew. He tells how Jesus got into the boat belonging to Simon Peter and from there taught the crowds that lined the shore. Then he describes Jesus' command to Peter to let down the nets one more time, in spite of Peter's protest that an entire night of fishing had produced nothing. After the miraculous catch of fish, which nearly sank two boats, Jesus said to Peter: 'Don't be afraid; from now on you will catch men' (5:10). The words 'from now on' emphasize the radical discontinuity with their former life. They are crossing a threshold. They are embarking on a life of apprenticeship, in preparation for a new vocation.

FLOCK (see also SHEEP)

Among Jesus' favourite descriptive terms for his followers were 'sheep' (*probaton*) and 'flock' (*poimne/poimnion*). He used these images to express the disciples' vulnerability to attack and their proneness to wander into danger, but also to affirm the depth of his sacrificial love for them in his role as the Good Shepherd.

In other New Testament passages which speak of the flock, the references to shepherds point to human leaders of congregations. In Acts 20:28,29, Paul urges the Ephesian elders to keep watch over 'all the flock', and to guard against the savage wolves that 'will not spare the flock'. In his first letter, likewise addressing elders, Peter urges them to 'be shepherds of God's flock', and to be 'examples to the flock' (1 Pet. 5:2,3). The first passage speaks of the sheep's need for protection; the second focuses on their need for instruction in right behaviour.

The image of the 'flock' also underscores the corporate nature of the Christian life. The shepherd attends to the needs of the individual sheep, but also deals with them as a group, leading them to pasture and protecting them from marauders.

FOLLOWER OF THE WAY

Several times in the book of Acts, Christianity is called 'the Way' (*hodos*), with Christians as 'followers of the Way'. Luke reports in Acts 9:2 that Saul had letters from the high priest so that he could imprison any in Damascus 'who belonged to the Way'. In Ephesus, Luke reports, some of the Jews 'refused to believe and publicly maligned the Way' (19:9); later, in the same city, 'there arose a great disturbance about the Way' (19:23). In Acts 22:4, speaking to the crowd in Jerusalem, Paul recalls his earlier life, and says, 'I persecuted the followers of this Way'. In his testimony before Felix, Paul says, 'I worship the God of our fathers, as a follower of the Way' (24:14); a few verses later Luke describes Felix as 'well acquainted with the Way' (24:22). This is a term, then, that believers chose for themselves, unlike 'Christian', which was coined for them.

A 'way' is a road or path. To describe Christianity as 'the Way' is to imply a distinctive manner of life, a pattern of behaviour, and also to imply a destination and a goal. The Christian life is not merely a pattern of belief, or an act of mental assent, but a framework for action. To be a follower of the Way is also to give exclusive allegiance to Jesus, who spoke of how 'narrow the road that leads to life' (Matthew 7:13,14), and who said, 'I am the way' (John 14:6).

FOUNDATION

In 1 Timothy 3:15, after giving instructions about the appointment of church leaders, Paul describes the community of believers as 'God's household, which is the church of the living God, the pillar and foundation (*hedraioma*) of the truth'. The truth of the gospel is committed to the church, the truth upon which all other truth must build. It is not simply one repository of truth among many truths, but it proclaims the truth in which is found the key to the unity of all of knowledge, whether historical, scientific, aesthetic, or philosophical.

Another word for foundation, *themelios*, is used of the foundation Paul laid for the church in Corinth, the one foundation which is Jesus Christ (1 Cor. 3:10–12); Paul uses the same word to describe the apostles and prophets as the foundation of the church in Ephesians 2:20. In 2 Timothy 2:19, when Paul says, 'God's solid foundation (*themelios*) stands firm', the reference may be again to the church, as in 1 Timothy 3:15.

FREEDMAN

The writings of Paul contain many allusions to our being set free from bondage and slavery. For example, in Romans 6, Paul says that we have been freed from slavery to sin in order to offer ourselves willingly as servants of God. In 1 Corinthians 8–10 he discusses the proper use of Christian freedom, as related to the treatment of the weaker brother. In Galatians 4 and 5 he contrasts bondage to the law with freedom to serve one another. And in Colossians 2 he calls for freedom from mere human regulations. However, the actual word for the slave who has been set free, 'freedman' (*apeleutheros*), occurs only in 1 Corinthians 7:22:

> He who was a slave when he was called by the Lord is the Lord's freedman (*apeleutheros*); similarly, he who was a free man (*eleutheros*) when he was called is Christ's slave.

Paul is explaining that no matter how enslaved a believer may be sociologically, there is still a far more fundamental freedom that he enjoys; on the other hand, no matter how free he may appear to be in the eyes of society, he is not free to do whatever he wants, but is responsible to the Lord as his master.

The other term used by Paul in this verse, 'free man' (*eleutheros*), refers to the person who was born free, who enjoys the full rights of citizenship in the Greek city-state. Peter uses the same word in his exhortation in 1 Peter 2:16, with the same caution to remember that even the one who is free is still Christ's servant: 'Live as free men (*eleutheroi*), but do not use your freedom as a cover-up for evil; live as servants of God.'

The language of freedom, slavery, and manumission provided vivid metaphors for first-century believers. Roman citizens often set their slaves free, and the freed slaves became Roman citizens, usually adopting the status of their former masters. When such slaves were free, they did not always leave their masters, but sometimes chose to remain as members of the family.

When the early Christians spoke of the believer as a 'free man' (*eleutheros*) or 'freedman' (*apeleutheros*), they employed terms that represented elevated status, with new dignity and privilege. Yet as Paul taught so clearly, no one was truly *born* free in the sense of the 'free man'. Rather, a person must be *set* free by the gracious act of God, thus becoming a 'freedman'. And somewhat as the manumitted slave might return to voluntarily serve in the *former* household, so the Christian had been set free to serve freely in the household of a *new* master, the Lord Jesus.

FRIEND

On two occasions Jesus refers to the disciples as his 'friends' (*philois*). The first is in Luke 12, while Jesus is making his way to Jerusalem. In a discourse warning his disciples about the hypocrisy of the Pharisees and the prospect of deadly persecution, he says: 'I tell you, my friends, do not be afraid of those who kill the body and after that can do no more' (12:4). Jesus does not use this form of address to the crowds, but only to those who are intimately associated with him in his sufferings. It is a term of affection, of love, derived from the verb 'to love' (*phileo*). It is a word that denotes companionship, closeness, camaraderie.

Jesus uses the same verb for 'love' (*phileo*) to describe the love of the Father for the Son (Jn. 5:20), the Father for the disciples (Jn. 16:27), and the disciples for Jesus (Jn. 16:27). But he also uses this word in reference to the love of family members for one another (Mt. 10:37) and the love of the Pharisees for positions of prominence (Mt. 23:6). Jesus employs the noun in several of his parables (e.g. Lk. 11:5–9; 15:3–10) and refers to Lazarus as 'our friend' (Jn. 11:11).

Thus the word 'friend' was part of Jesus' vocabulary long before the Last Supper, and included references to his followers. But not until John 15 does Jesus draw out the full meaning of the word, applying it to his relationship to the disciples. Here, after repeating the great new commandment, 'Love each other as I have loved you' (15:12; cf. 13:34,35), Jesus affirms that the greatest demonstration of love (*agape*) is that one lay down his life for his friends (15:13). So then the discussion of friendship is set in the context of the highest expression of love (*agape*).

Jesus says to his disciples:

> You are my friends if you do what I command. I no longer call you servants, because a servant does not know his master's business. Instead, I have called you friends, for everything that I learned from my Father I have made known to you (15:14,15).

Here Jesus expresses what may seem to be a surprising dimension of friendship, at least in those cultures where friendship is seen as a peer relationship, a reciprocal term that carries no hint of hierarchy or inequality. Jesus announces that the test of true friendship is the disciples' willingness to *obey* his commands and, specifically, the command to love one another. Similarly, in verse 10, Jesus says that just as he demonstrates his love for the Father by obedience to the Father's commands, so the disciples must demonstrate their love for Jesus by obeying Jesus' commands.

Thus the essence of friendship lies not in the abolition of authority, or in the removal of role distinctions, but rather in the appropriate expression of love. And when one is under the authority of another the most appropriate expression of love, and hence friendship, is obedience.

The servant and the friend of Jesus are alike in that both have the obligation to obey. However, they are different in that the servant does not know his master's business. The master owes the servant no reasons or justifications. But Jesus made known to the disciples everything that he had heard from the Father – all the context, the reasons, the purposes for acting as he did.

When Jesus says, 'I no longer call you servants', he is not saying that the relationship of servanthood has ceased, that the disciples should not call themselves Jesus' servants, or that he will no longer refer to himself as Master (cf. Jn. 13:13). Rather, he is saying that 'servant' is no longer an adequate metaphor to convey all the dimensions of intimacy that the disciples have come to enjoy with Jesus. Nothing less than the word 'friend' will do to express the richness of communication and love that have come to characterize the relationship.

Apart from Jesus' use of the term, and other occurrences of the word in ordinary social usage (e.g. officials in Ephesus described as 'friends' of Paul, Acts 19:31), the only appearance of 'friend' (*philos*) as a term for Christians comes in

John's third letter. In his closing remarks, John says, 'The friends here send their greetings. Greet the friends there by name' (v. 14). It is interesting that the gospel writer who records Jesus' statement, 'I have called you friends' (Jn. 15:15), should also be the New Testament writer to use this term for his fellow-disciples. With this word he expresses the love (*philia*, *phileo*), the bond of companionship and shared life in community, that ties believers together.

G

GUARDIAN

The 'guardian' (*paidogogos*), was a servant who acted as the custodian or guide for the children. His role was to conduct the children to and from school, and respect was due to him as well as to the father. In Galatians 3:24,25, Paul describes the Law as a guardian conducting us to Christ. In 1 Corinthians 4:15,16, he uses the image in a different way: 'Even though you have ten thousand guardians in Christ, you do not have many fathers, for in Christ Jesus I became your father through the gospel. Therefore I urge you to imitate me.' The Corinthians had had many who had assisted them and watched over them in their Christian life as guardians, leaders who had come along after Paul, some as eminent as Peter and Apollos. But there remained a special relationship with the one who had brought them to birth.

GUEST OF THE BRIDEGROOM

Jesus introduces the metaphor of the guest of the bridegroom in answering a question about why his disciples, unlike the disciples of John the Baptist and the Pharisees, do not fast. He replies: 'How can the guests of the bridegroom (*hoi hyioi tou nymphonos*) mourn while he is with them? The time will come when the bridegroom will be taken from them; then they will fast' (Mt. 9:15; cf. Mk. 2:19; Lk. 5:34). Although the three gospel writers employ slightly different wording, all use the phrase 'guest of the bridegroom'.

This image is one of joy, of celebration in the midst of companions. But the focal point is the bridegroom, who represents Jesus. The guests are derivative and subordinate. They have no role apart from the bridegroom. Their function is to keep the celebration focused on him and to share in his joy.

The wedding imagery is found in two other parables recorded by Matthew. In Matthew 22:1–14 (cf. Lk. 14:16–24), the parable of the wedding banquet, the king's invited guests refuse to come, and even mistreat the messengers. So the king sends out his servants into the streets in order to fill the wedding hall with guests. Those who are invited include both good and bad. They are distinguished only by their willingness to respond to the invitation. They have no other qualifications. Jesus uses this illustration to picture his followers as those who have been included in the community of celebration solely by the gracious act of God, not through any merit of their own.

In Matthew 25:1–13, the image of the wedding banquet appears once again in the parable of the ten virgins. Those who are allowed to enter are the ones who took along extra oil and therefore were able to keep their lamps burning when the arrival of the bridegroom was later than expected. Here again the disciples are compared to participants in a wedding celebration. They are to stay on the alert, prepared for their master's return at any moment.

H

HEIR

An aspect of membership in God's family cited several times by the New Testament writers is the promise of an inheritance. To be God's child is also to be his 'heir' (*kleronomos*; Gal. 3:2; 4:7). In this position of privilege we are identified with Christ, says Paul, as 'fellow-heirs' (*synkleronomoi*, Rom. 8:17). This privilege is extended to the Gentiles together with Israel (Eph. 3:6). The poor of this world, James reminds us, have been chosen by God to be heirs of the kingdom (Jas. 2:15). Husbands, says Peter, are to treat their wives with sensitivity, realizing that they are 'heirs with you of the gracious gift of life' (1 Pet. 3:7).

Jesus also uses the image of the heir in his parables (Mt. 21:38; Mk. 12:7; Lk. 20:14), but not to describe his disciples. Rather, he pictures himself as the rightful heir who is rejected and killed by the tenants of the vineyard. However, Jesus does use the related verb 'inherit' (*kleronomeo*) in reference to his disciples: 'Blessed are the meek, for they will inherit the earth' (Mt. 5:5); 'Come, you who are blessed by my Father; take your inheritance, the

kingdom prepared for you since the creation of the world'
(Mt. 25:34); 'Everyone who has left houses or brothers or
sisters or father or mother or children or fields for my sake
will receive a hundred times as much and will inherit
eternal life' (Mt. 19:29).

HERALD

In classical Greek, the 'herald' (*keryx*) was a messenger
commissioned by his ruler or the state to announce some
item of news. He was used to announce judicial verdicts.
Twice Paul applies this metaphor to himself, saying that
God had appointed him as 'a herald' (1 Tim. 2:7; 2 Tim.
1:11). The corresponding verb is used of Jesus in Mark 1:14:
'Jesus went into Galilee, proclaiming (*kerusson*) the good
news of God.'

The herald delivers a message on behalf of someone else.
He does not make up his own announcements, but rather
functions under the authority of the one who sent him.

HOUSEHOLD, MEMBER OF THE

In Matthew 10, Jesus gives instructions to the twelve before
sending them out. He speaks of the persecutions that the
disciples will encounter as they go into the world as his
witnesses, and he warns them that they can expect no better
treatment than he has received himself. He then cites three
role pairs, each expressing inequality of status and authority:
student with teacher, servant with master, and members of
the household with the head of the house. Jesus, the head
of the household, has been called Beelzebub, the prince of

demons. The disciples, as 'members of the household', can therefore expect even worse treatment (Mt. 10:24,25).

This metaphor expresses both connection and inequality. On the one hand, the disciples are members of the household, with all the associated rights and privileges. On the other hand, their role is defined in relation to the head of the house. They are under his authority, and responsible to him for their tasks. They are not his peers, even though they share a common life.

Although the noun translated 'member of a household' (*oikiakos*) (Mt. 10:25) occurs only once in the gospels, the synonymous term *oikeios*, as well as the root term *oikos* (house, household), are very prominent in the remainder of the New Testament. The 'household' was the most important and fundamental structure of the Hellenistic world. Neither Hebrew nor Greek have a word for the nuclear family as we know it today, with parents and children living together as an isolated unit. Rather, the basic form of social organization was the household, which consisted of not only the immediate family, but also various combinations of slaves, freedmen, friends, clients, labourers, business associates and tenants, as well as other relatives, all under the authority of the 'head of the household', the senior male member of the most prominent family.

In order to understand the associations of this image for first-century Christians, it is important to appreciate the strong bonds of solidarity and loyalty that tied members of a household together. Participation in the common history of the head of a family was even more important than biological descent in bonding society together. Members of a household would embrace whichever religion had been chosen by the head of the house (e.g. Cornelius, Acts 11:14; Lydia, 16:15; Philippian jailer, 16:31; Chrispus, 18:8).

In his letter to the Galatians, Paul reminds them of the special obligations and loyalty they owe to one another as members of the 'family (*oikeious*) of believers' (Gal. 6:10). He uses the same word in Ephesians to tell Jews and Gentiles that Christ has overcome the estrangement and hostility that formerly kept them apart: 'You are . . . fellow-citizens with God's people and members of God's household' (Eph. 2:19). To be a member of God's household is to belong, to be related, to be intimately interconnected.

In giving instructions to Timothy about the qualifications of church leaders, Paul says that a person's leadership in the home demonstrates fitness for leadership in the church. With this parallel fresh in mind, Paul explains that that he has written about these matters so that 'you will know how people ought to conduct themselves in God's household, which is the church of the living God' (1 Tim. 3:15).

Other New Testament writers also refer to the community of believers as God's household. Twice the author of Hebrews describes Jesus as presiding over God's 'house' (*oikos*) – first, as Son (Heb. 3:6), and then as high priest (Heb. 10:21). In his first letter, Peter warns Christians that, 'It is time for judgement to begin with the family (*oikou*) of God' (1 Pet. 4:17).

Although the first-century household was broader than the nuclear family as we know it today, the terms most commonly used in the New Testament to describe the relationships between believers were drawn from the innermost circle of relationships – brother, sister, father, mother, son, and daughter.

I

IMITATOR

In Ephesians 5:1, Paul urges the Ephesian believers to 'be imitators (*mimetai*) of God . . . as dearly loved children'; specifically, he exhorts them to demonstrate the self-sacrificing love of Christ. The idea of imitation naturally arises from the image of a child following in the footsteps of a parent.

Another dimension of this imitation is introduced in Paul's first letter to the Corinthians where he says, 'I urge you to imitate me' (4:16), and, 'Follow my example, as I follow the example of Christ' (11:1). In Philippians 3:17, Paul invites the church to 'join with others in following my example'. Twice he commends the Thessalonian believers for their willingness to imitate the example of other believers as well as the Lord: 'you became imitators of us and of the Lord' (1 Thess. 1:6), and 'you, brothers, became imitators of God's churches in Judea' (1 Thess. 2:14).

Paul invited imitation only from those who were his spiritual children. He did not expect the believers to imitate him in all his personal idiosyncracies, but only in those respects in which he was modelling the character and mission of Jesus Christ.

Paul's use of the term 'imitator' corresponds to Jesus' call to become a 'disciple' or 'learner' (*mathetes*). In this way the importance of learning from human role models is not overlooked, but the central allegiance remains focused on Jesus Christ.

INFANT (see CHILD)

L

LAND

In Hebrews 6:7–8 the author pictures two types of land (*ge*). As in Jesus' parable of the soils, the contrast is between land that produces and land that does not. Both drink in the rain that falls on them; and both are intended to be useful to those for whom they are being farmed. In the first case, the land produces a useful crop and receives the blessing of God. But in the second case, the land produces only thorns and thistles; it is worthless, in danger of being cursed (though still not abandoned as utterly worthless), and in the end is burned (a common farmer's solution for dealing with a weed-infested field, in order to prepare it for the next planting season). Similarly, the believer receives blessings from God for a purpose; he or she is expected to produce something useful for the Lord with these resources and opportunities; something of value is supposed to grow in and through his or her life.

LEADER

A term for leader used mainly by the author of Hebrews is *hegemonos*, a present participle based on the verb *hegeomai* (to lead or guide). In Luke 22:26, Jesus says to his disciples, 'the greatest among you should be like the youngest, and the one who rules (*hegemonòs*) like the one who serves'. The term 'leader' (*hegemonos*) is used of kings of Israel (Ezek. 43:7), military commanders (1 Macc. 9:30; 2 Macc. 14:16), rulers of Judah (Mt. 2:6), and Joseph's position as ruler of Egypt (Acts 7:10). Thus it is a word used for broad and authoritative leadership roles. In Acts 15:22, Judas and Silas, chosen to help convey the decisions of the Jerusalem Council to the Gentile believers, are described as 'leaders (*hegoumenous*) among the brothers'; thus, even among 'brothers' there can be leaders; the fact that all are brothers does not invalidate the leadership function within the community.

In the last chapter of the book of Hebrews, the author refers to the role of leader three times. The leaders are described as those 'who spoke the word of God to you' (13:7), that is, those who first preached and established churches among them. In the first place, the believers are exhorted to 'remember' their leaders, to 'consider the outcome of their way of life', and to 'imitate their faith' (13:7); the leaders in view here are primarily teachers and role models. Second, they are told to 'obey' their leaders and to 'submit to their authority' with willing spirits that will enable the leaders to do their work with joy (13:17). In this case, the leaders are described as those who 'keep watch over you'; these may or may not be the same leaders who originally brought the word of God to them, but the leadership role described here seems to imply the general supervisory role implied in the word 'ruler' in the other contexts already cited. Finally, the author instructs his readers to 'greet' their leaders as well as all God's people (13:24); thus the 'leaders' are an identifiable group, distinguishable from the membership of the community as a whole. Notice that 'leader' always occurs in the plural when the reference is to a particular local situation. The picture we see in the New Testament is of a team of individuals working together, not of one strong individual dominating all the others.

Another set of words denoting leadership in the New Testament writings is based on the verb *prohistemi*, the basic meaning of which is to set before or over someone or something. In secular Greek the participle *prohistamenos* was used to refer to leadership in an army, a state, or a party. In various contexts it included ideas of guarding, protecting, supporting, and caring.

Paul uses this word a number of times in reference to church leadership. He exhorts the Thessalonians to 'respect those who work hard among you, who are over (*prohistamenous*) you in the Lord and who admonish you', and to 'hold them in the highest regard in love because of their work' (1 Thess. 5:12,13). In 1 Timothy 5:17 he urges proper respect and/or compensation for elders who 'direct (*proestotes*) the affairs of the church well'.

In reviewing the qualifications for overseers and deacons in 1 Timothy 3, Paul says that the ability to lead a household is an important indicator of ability to lead in the church. Paul insists that the overseer must 'manage (*prohistamenon*) his own family well and see that his children obey him with proper respect' (v. 4), for 'If anyone does not know how to manage (*prostenai*) his own family, how can he take care of God's church?' (v. 5). Similarly, the deacon must demonstrate the ability to 'manage (*prohistamenoi*) his children and his household well' (v. 12). The word 'manage/lead' (*prohistemi*) plainly carries a note of authority, as well as indicating the demonstration of personal care. Both respect and obedience are expected from those who are under the direction of the leader.

In Romans 12, Paul urges the believers to exercise the capacities Christ has given to them. He lists seven spiritual gifts, of which the sixth is leadership: 'if it is leadership (*ho prohistamenos*), let him govern diligently' (v. 8). Note that leadership is seen as a gift of the Spirit, not simply an office to which one is elected or appointed.

LETTER

In 2 Corinthians 3:1–3, Paul pictures those believers as a letter (*epistole*) of recommendation written from Christ, by Paul, with the Holy Spirit, on the hearts of Paul and Timothy. It is an open letter, displayed for anyone to read, providing proof of the authenticity of Paul's ministry in that the letter describes lives that have been changed by the gospel. Christ is the author of the letter; Paul is only the scribe. The point of the illustration is that the very existence and life of the Corinthian church gives public evidence to the power of Christ, and to the effectiveness of the apostolic ministry.

In choosing this image, Paul was drawing on a very familiar practice in the first-century world. Letter writing was such a common means of communication that standard formats were developed for various kinds of letters. The letters were often written by secretaries, and were sent through slaves, friends, and even strangers who happened to be travelling in the right direction.

LIGHT

In the well-known passage from the Sermon on the Mount, Jesus addresses his disciples thus: 'You are the light (*phos*) of the world' (Mt. 5:14). The purpose of the light is to be *seen*, so that people will be drawn to praise their Father in heaven. The disciples are to be like a city on the top of a hill, and like a lamp put on its stand, not hidden under a bowl (5:14–16).

Each aspect of this metaphor speaks of widely dispersed influence. The disciples are to be a light for the *world*. They are intended to radiate like a lamp to everyone in the house. Their light is meant to shine before men. The disciples, in other words, are supposed to have an impact on others, drawing them to glorify and praise the Lord. That is their fundamental ministry task. The light, says Jesus, consists of their good deeds. Thus their primary influence is that of setting an outstanding example.

Jesus identifies his followers with light in a couple of other passages as well. In Luke 16:8, in the parable of the shrewd manager, Jesus alludes to the 'people of the light', and in John 12:36 he urges the crowd in Jerusalem: 'Put your trust in the light while you have it, so that you may become sons of light.'

Similarly, Paul reminds the Thessalonian believers: 'You are all sons of the light and sons of the day' (1 Thess. 5:5), and that therefore they should be alert, self-controlled, and ready for Christ's coming. He exhorts the Ephesians: 'You were once darkness, but now you are light in the Lord. Live as children of light' (5:8). In the following verse Paul explains what that life of 'light' involves: goodness, righteousness, and truth. Continuing the metaphor, he urges them to expose the darkness of the world around them

(5:11–14), bringing hidden things into the light. Thus the image of light is not only a symbol of the moral purity to which Christians are called, but also a call to confront the world with the reality of God's truth.

The same combination of the call to moral purity and the summons to proclaim God's truth to the world is conveyed by Paul's use of the image of the star (*phoster*) in Philippians 2:

> Do everything without complaining or arguing, so that you may become blameless and pure, children of God without fault in a crooked and depraved generation, in which you shine like stars (*phosteres*) in the universe as you hold out the word of life (2:14–16).

M

Manager

Only once does Jesus use the metaphor of manager to describe his followers. However, in the parable of the shrewd manager, recorded in Luke 16:1–12, Jesus provides a vivid description of the function of the manager (*oikonomos*). In that parable a rich man has a manager who is in charge of his possessions. The manager is accountable to the rich man, and his effectiveness is measured by how well he invests the resources in ways that benefit the rich man. If the manager is found guilty of wasting the owner's resources, he will be put out of his job. The manager has considerable freedom to negotiate with the various people who owe money to the rich man. In this parable, the manager is commended for his shrewdness in using material resources to accomplish his goals, not for his dishonesty in the process. Jesus uses the shrewd manager to illustrate the importance of good stewardship in handling material possessions and in managing that which belongs to another. But in this story, the shrewd manager himself is not used as an image for the disciple.

Yet in Luke 12 Jesus does use a manager as an illustration of a disciple. There Jesus is speaking of the importance of being ready for his return and of making good use of resources in the light of the coming judgement. He introduces a short parable: 'Who then is the faithful and wise manager, whom the master puts in charge of his servants to give them their food allowance at the proper time?' (12:42). The manager who does what he is supposed to do will be rewarded by being placed in charge of all the master's possessions (12:44). But the one who abuses the menservants and maidservants, and who indulges himself in gluttony and drunkenness, will be punished.

Thus the manager is one who holds a position of responsibility. He can be in charge of people as well as possessions. But notice that in verses 43, 45, and 46 the manager is referred to as 'servant'. That is, he occupies a position of authority, but he also remains *under* authority.

Other New Testament writers employ the image of the manager as well. In 1 Corinthians 4:2–4, Paul mentions that the most important qualification for the manager is faithfulness, and that only the Lord has the right to evaluate who has been faithful and who has not. When listing the qualifications for an overseer in the church, Paul says that since the overseer is entrusted with God's work (*hos theou oikonomon*), that is, since he functions as a steward or manager, he must be blameless (Tit. 1:7). In each case we see the strong emphasis on accountability that underlies all of the servant words, and especially the manager/steward image.

Although the two passages mentioned above use the manager metaphor for Christian leaders (apostles and overseers), Peter chooses the term for an exhortation intended for all of his readers: 'Each one should use whatever gift he has received to serve others, faithfully administering (*hos kaloi oikonomoi*) God's grace in its various forms' (1 Pet. 4:10). Thus Peter sees each Christian as a manager, equally responsible to make use of the gifts and ministry opportunities that God has provided.

A large household could have more than one manager or steward, with separate managers over the cooks, the estate, the accounts, and so forth. Thus we can appreciate why Peter could speak of each Christian as a 'steward', because each one carried a certain amount of leadership responsibility within God's household, implied in the gift assigned to him or her.

MIST

An image that reminds us of our vulnerability and weakness appears once in James: 'You are a mist (*atmis*) that appears for a little while and then vanishes' (4:14). In view of the brevity and uncertainty of life, says James, we should not boast about our plans for the future, but should humbly acknowledge that, 'If it is the Lord's will, we will live and do this or that' (4:15). This is an appropriate caution, especially in view of the popularity in some quarters of the image of the Christian leader as the person who 'makes things happen', the manager or administrator who plans, organizes, and directs the community into the future. We must remember that the leader too is only a 'mist', here for a little while, then gone, dependent entirely on the grace of God for every breath.

MODEL

The original meaning of 'model' (*typos*) is that of a form, and in particular a hollow mould, which leaves an impression when pressed against another object. This word is found in several of the New Testament letters in reference to believers setting a pattern of life for others to imitate. Paul commends the Thessalonians for becoming imitators of the apostles and the Lord, and subsequently becoming 'a model to all the believers in Macedonia and Achaia' (1 Thess. 1:7), known for their faith and for their decisive turning from idols to God. In his second letter to them, Paul recalls how he and his team worked constantly in order to provide for their own needs, 'in order to make ourselves a model for you to follow' (2 Thess. 3:9); the need for such a model is evident from the surrounding verses, in which Paul rebukes those who are unwilling to work for a living (3:6,11–12).

Paul invites the Philippian believers: 'Join with others in following my example, brothers, and take note of those who live according to the pattern (*typon*) we gave you' (3:17). Similarly, he urges Timothy, though he is relatively young, to 'set an example (*typos*) for the believers' (1 Tim. 4:12), and Titus also to set an example for the young men in everything, by doing what is good (Tit. 2:7). Peter encourages the elders not to be domineering in their leadership, but rather to be 'examples (*typoi*) to the flock' (1 Pet. 5:3). Each of these passages highlights the special responsibility of the spiritual leader to set the pace, and to provide a pattern of life that is worthy of imitation.

MOTHER (see FATHER / MOTHER)

N

NATION

In describing followers of Christ, Peter says in 1 Peter 2:9–11:

> But you are a chosen people, a royal priesthood, a holy nation (*ethnos*), a people belonging to God, that you may declare the praises of him who called you out of darkness into his wonderful light. Once you were not a people, but now you are the people of God; once you had not received mercy, but now you have received mercy.

The reference to believers as a holy nation is taken from Exodus 19:6. A 'nation' (*ethnos*) is a group of people held together by common customs and patterns of life. The church, too, is a people set apart, distinct from others. Although not physically or geographically separated, their habits and behaviour should make clear that they belong specially to God, reserved for his service. To become a Christian, then, is in a sense to adopt a new 'culture', with a new worldview, a new system of values, and a new pattern of behaviour.

This image of God's people as a nation is used briefly by Jesus in Matthew 21:43, where he says: 'Therefore I tell you that the kingdom of God will be taken away from you and given to a people (*ethnei*) who will produce its fruit.' Such a statement must have been quite startling to Jesus' Jewish listeners, who referred to Israel as the people of God, while all the rest of mankind were called the 'nations' (*ethne*).

NEIGHBOUR

The term 'neighbour' (*plesion*) is somewhat vague, connected with the word 'near' (*pelas*). It calls to mind the image of the one living next to me in community.

In most of the passages where 'neighbour' appears in the New Testament letters, the context deals with the treatment of fellow-believers, rather than the Christian's witness to the unbelieving community. In Romans 15:2, Paul summarizes his discussion about the strong and weak members of the fellowship by exhorting his readers: 'Each of us should please his neighbour for his good, to build him up.' 'Neighbour' is a word that bridges a barrier; it reminds us that we are near to someone from whom we might feel distant. Similarly in Ephesians 4:25, Paul rebukes the practice of lying on the basis that we are connected to one another: 'Each of you must put off falsehood and speak truthfully to his neighbour, for we are all members of one body.' James rebukes his readers for their attitudes of favouritism within the congregation, quoting the commandment, 'Love your neighbour as yourself' (2:8). Later in his letter he deals with the problem of a judgemental spirit toward fellow-believers, asking,

'But you – who are you to judge your neighbour?' (4:12). Thus to be a neighbour is to be closely connected in God's eyes; and, therefore, we have no right to push one another away.

O

Overseer

In secular Greek the noun 'overseer' is used to describe a deity keeping watch over a country (especially concerning treaties and markets), men with responsible positions with the state, and officials of religious communities. The verb 'oversee' (*episkopeo*) stresses active and responsible care. It implies overall supervising, ordering, evaluating, and setting of direction.

The word 'overseer' (*episkopos*) is applied to leaders within the church fellowship. The letter to the Philippians is addressed to 'all the saints in Christ Jesus at Philippi, together with the overseers and deacons' (1:1). In 1 Timothy 3:1, Paul says that 'If anyone sets his heart on being an overseer, he desires a noble task', and then lists the qualifications that should be expected of an overseer. A similar list for the overseer's qualifications is given in Titus 1, where the terms 'overseer' and 'elder' (*presbyteros*) are used for the same person (1:5,7).

In both Acts 20 and 1 Peter 5, it is evident that the three primary terms for church leader (elder, overseer, shepherd/pastor) were used interchangeably in the early church. In Acts 20, Paul is addressing the elders of the church at Ephesus (v. 17); he charges them to 'guard yourselves and all the flock of which the Holy Spirit has made you overseers', and to 'be shepherds of the church of God' (20:28). All three terms describe the same set of leaders. In the same way, in his first letter Peter addresses elders (5:1) and urges them to 'be shepherds of God's flock that is under your care, serving as overseers' (5:2).

P

PARENT (see FATHER / MOTHER)

PARTNER

The word 'partner' (*koinonos*) occurs in Luke 5:10 in connection with James and John, who were partners with Simon Peter in the fishing business. 'Partner' also occurs in Revelation 18:4 where the followers of Jesus are warned to disassociate themselves from Babylon, the wicked trade centre that symbolizes the world system, and not to be a 'partner' with her in her sins. Both of these passages illustrate the secular and commercial associations that help us to see the implications of this image.

Underlying the whole word group that includes 'partner' (*koinonos*) and the frequently occurring 'fellowship' (*koinonia*) is the phenomenon of voluntary associations in the Hellenistic world. People who had a common interest, a social or philanthropic cause, a trade or a philosophy would band together into a voluntary association. All of these associations had a religious dimension. They provided their participants with a depth of personal relationship and a sense of identity, based not on similar social status or background but on common goals. Their functions included common meals, caring for one another in sickness, and helping with burial expenses. In fact, the bonds formed were so close that sometimes the authorities became uneasy about the potential power of these associations and banned them.

The parallels with the first-century Christian fellowships are obvious. When the apostles Paul and John spoke of partnership with fellow-Christians, they were invoking one of the most powerful images of intimate, interdependent relationship known in the world of their day. Paul describes Titus as 'my partner and fellow-worker among you' (2 Cor. 8:23), and appeals to Philemon to welcome Onesimus by saying, 'if you consider me a partner' (Philem. 17). In the book of Revelation, the author John identifies himself as 'your brother and companion (*synkoinonos*) in the suffering and kingdom and patient endurance that are ours in Jesus' (Rev. 1:9).

PATRONESS/HELPER

In Romans 16:2, Paul sends greetings to Phoebe, saying, 'she has been a great help (*prostatis*) to many people, including me'. The word *prostatis* means protectress, patroness, helper, and corresponds to the masculine *prostates*, which was found in both Jewish and pagan religious circles. In this context, the term does not denote authoritative leadership, but rather a ministry of generous care for the congregation.

PEOPLE

'People' (*laos*) is the word reserved in the Greek Old Testament for Israel as the people specially chosen by God. Israel is a people solely by God's gracious initiative, not by any merit of their own. In 1 Peter 2:9–11, Peter employs this term to describe followers of Christ:

> But you are a chosen people, a royal priesthood, a holy nation, a people (*laos*) belonging to God, that you may declare the praises of him who called you out of darkness into his wonderful light. Once you were not a people (*laos*), but now you are the people of God; once you had not received mercy, but now you have received mercy.

Three other New Testament authors use this image as well. Insisting upon the necessity of the Christian's separation from everything that is evil, Paul combines three Old Testament passages (Lev. 26:12; Jer. 32:38; Ezek. 37:27) that speak of God's relationship to his people: 'As God has said: "I will live with them and walk among them, and I will be their God, and they will be my people" ' (2 Cor. 6:16). The author of Hebrews speaks about the Sabbath rest that remains for the people of God (Heb. 4:9). Then, finally, the promise of being God's people finds its fulfilment in the magnificent vision of John in the book of Revelation: 'They will be his people, and God himself will be with them and be their God' (21:3).

PILLAR

In 1 Timothy 3:15, after giving instructions about the appointment of church leaders, Paul describes the community of believers as 'God's household, which is the church of the living God, the pillar (*stylos*) and foundation of the truth'. To the church is committed the truth of the gospel, upon which all other truth must build.

In Galatians 2, Paul uses this word 'pillar' (*stylos*) for individual leaders of the Jerusalem church. When describing his visit to Jerusalem to explain his ministry among the Gentiles, Paul says that he met privately with 'those who seemed to be leaders' (Gal. 2:2). A few verses later he says that 'those who seemed to be important' (2:6) added nothing to his message. Then, in verse 9, he reports that 'James, Peter and John, those reputed to be pillars (*styloi*), gave me and Barnabas the right hand of fellowship when they recognised the grace given to me.' A pillar holds up the building; the whole structure depends on the pillars. However, Paul's reluctance to say that Peter, James, and John really *were* 'pillars' is shown in his usage three times of the verb 'seemed' or 'reputed' (*dokeo*). His reluctance to overstate the importance of the roles of these leaders in Jerusalem must be understood in the context of the dispute that occasioned both his trip to Jerusalem and his later letter to the Galatians; for, in the matter of understanding that the gospel abolished all walls between Jew and Gentile, Paul was apparently farther advanced than the Jerusalem church and its leaders. No church leaders should ever be elevated so high by the congregation that they rise above the possibility of correction and rebuke. Nor should any individual leader ever become such a 'pillar' to a congregation that his or her removal would mean the collapse of the whole building.

The term 'pillar' also appears in the promise of the Spirit of Jesus to the overcomer in Revelation 3:12: 'Him who overcomes I will make a pillar in the temple of my God.'

PILOT

A very colourful leadership word, used only once in the New Testament, is 'administration' (*kybernesis*), based on the word *kybernetes*, which means the captain, pilot, or steersman of a ship. In 1 Corinthians 12 Paul is listing the spiritual gifts that God has appointed in the church. First he cites apostles, prophets, and teachers as a group; after that he lists 'workers of miracles, also those having gifts of healing, those able to help others, those with gifts of administration (*kyberneseis*), and those speaking in different kinds of tongues' (12:28).

The related verb, 'to pilot' (*kybernao*) probably came at first from the language used by Mediterranean sailors; but very early it came to be used in a metaphorical sense as well. In the Greek Old Testament, 'administration' or 'piloting' is given as the function of rulers (Prov. 1:5; 11:14).

In the New Testament, 'pilot' occurs at Acts 27:11 and Revelation 18:17 as the one who steers the ship, who brings it to its destination. This person's responsibilities, of course, would include the direction of the activities of the other crew members. From Acts 27:11 it is clear that the owner of the ship and the pilot are two different people. This observation contributes a useful insight into the illustration: the owner of the ship determines where it is to go, but the pilot determines the best route and method to get there. In the same way, the overall goal of the church has been defined by the Lord, the 'owner'; but the role of the administrator, the 'ship's captain', is to establish the specific direction and to co-ordinate the activities of the other members toward that end.

PLANTING, NEW

In 1 Timothy 3:6, Paul warns Timothy that the person appointed as overseer must not be a 'recent convert'. Literally, he must not be a 'new planting' (*neophytos*), like a tender young tree just set into the soil. A young believer must have opportunity to grow, to develop strength, to attain some measure of maturity. The ability to bear good fruit must be demonstrated. If such growth has not had time to occur, there is considerable risk that the appointment to leadership will foster pride and will make the new believer vulnerable to spiritual attack (3:6). Potential leaders need time to grow.

POSSESSION

The word 'treasure' is based on the Hebrew word *segullah*, which refers to personal property, and in particular, to a king's treasure (David's 'personal treasures of gold and silver' in 1 Chronicles 29:3; Solomon's 'treasure of kings and provinces' in Ecclesiastes 2:8). This is the word which the Lord used to describe Israel as his treasured possession (e.g. Exod. 19:5; Deut. 7:6; 14:2; 26:18; Mal. 3:17). Most often it is translated in the Greek Old Testament as 'rich possession' (*periousios*), but sometimes as 'possession, property' (*peripoiesis*). Both Greek words are used by New Testament writers to describe the special relationship of God to his people.

In Ephesians Paul describes the Holy Spirit as a seal, 'a deposit guaranteeing our inheritance until the redemption of those who are God's possession (*peripoieseos*)' (1:14). The whole passage is filled with descriptions of the riches and privileges that are ours in Jesus Christ, because of God's love and gracious choice. In the second chapter of his first letter, where he lists all the terms formerly descriptive of Israel but now applied to Christians, Peter says that believers are 'a people belonging to God (*laos eis peripoiesin*)' (1 Pet. 2:9). Several times in this letter, written to Christians who were suffering insults and ostracism from their society, Peter speaks of God's choosing them, and uses terms like this to remind them of their value in the eyes of God. In Titus 2:14, Paul employs a similar term, 'rich possession' (*periousios*), reminding Titus that Jesus Christ 'gave himself for us to redeem us from all wickedness and to purify for himself a people that are his very own (*laon periousion*), eager to do what is good'.

PRIEST

The image of 'priest' is not used by Jesus, and is referred to only indirectly by Paul, yet it has become one of the most important, and most controversial images, in the later history of the church.

The book of Exodus introduces the idea of the corporate priesthood of the entire nation of Israel even before the appointment of the first Levitical priests. At the foot of Mount Sinai, before the giving of the ten commandments, God says to his people: 'You will be for me a kingdom of priests and a holy nation' (Exod. 19:6). The same promise is extended to Israel regathered by the Messiah in the Year of Jubilee, as pictured by Isaiah: 'You will be called priests of the LORD, you will be named ministers of our God' (61:6). Although the majority of references in the Old Testament concerning priests are specifically to the sons of

Aaron and to their duties related to the tabernacle and the temple, these two passages speak of a more general function of standing between God and the rest of mankind which is part of their call to be a 'holy nation'.

When the New Testament writers speak of 'priests' and 'priesthood', they are referring to privileges that belong to all of God's people, not just to an elite group of leaders or liturgical functionaries. In fact, given the great importance of the priestly functions in Israel's spiritual life, as well as the large number of priests and temples in the Hellenistic cities, it is remarkable that the writers of the New Testament did *not* make greater use of these metaphors. We must conclude that it was not a matter of oversight, but of conscious avoidance.

No individual in the New Testament is ever called a 'priest'. The metaphor is always used in a corporate sense. Its most extended development is found in 1 Peter 2. There Peter begins by describing believers as living stones being built together into a spiritual house, but then changes the image: 'to be a holy priesthood (*hierateuma*), offering spiritual sacrifices acceptable to God through Jesus Christ' (2:5). In the next few verses he develops the metaphor of Jesus Christ as the cornerstone, and then returns in verse 9 to the theme of priesthood, quoting from Exodus 19 and other Old Testament passages: 'But you are a chosen people, a royal priesthood (*hierateuma*), a holy nation, a people belonging to God, that you may declare the praises of him who called you out of darkness into his wonderful light.' The privileges of leading in worship, and of offering sacrifice, usually reserved for the priests, now belong to all of God's people. Nor are these functions given to a special class of people within the church. The image of priesthood is not used to imply special authority for the leader, or restricted performance of liturgical ceremonies, or any unusual measure of personal consecration or holiness. Rather, the privileges described are open to all.

The book of Revelation also employs the image of priest on several occasions in describing the privileged position made available to Christians. In Revelation 1:6, John describes Jesus Christ as the one who 'has made us to be a kingdom and priests to serve his God and Father'. Note that this priesthood is by God's appointment; in this context it is not a hereditary office nor a task for which one volunteers.

Again, in Revelation 5:9,10 the four living creatures and the twenty-four elders sing praise to the Lamb:

> You are worthy to take the scroll
>   and to open its seals,
> because you were slain,
>   and with your blood you
>   purchased men for God
>   from every tribe and language and
>   people and nation.
> You have made them to be a kingdom
>   and priests to serve our God,
>   and they will reign on the earth.

In view of the explicit mention of people from every tribe, language, people, and nation, it is clear that this new priesthood is not just for the exclusive few – not for the descendants of one priest, Aaron, or for one tribe, Levi, or even for one nation, Israel. The extraordinary value ascribed by God to the entire priestly people is implied by the price that was paid for them – the Lamb's own blood.

This section of Revelation also highlights another aspect of the priestly function – to share in God's rule, just as the priests taught the Law to God's people and helped to order the life of the community accordingly. Although all are on the same level as priests, this equality is not inconsistent with the exercise of authority (although the authority in view here is not authority within the community, but authority that will be exercised over the created order and/or over the unbelieving world). Once again, in Revelation 20:6, the idea of priesthood is associated with the function of ruling:

> Blessed and holy are those who have part in the first resurrection. The second death has no power over them, but they will be priests of God and of Christ and will reign with him for a thousand years.

The words 'blessed' and 'holy' underscore the themes of joy and privilege that are associated with this priesthood.

PROPHET

The role of the 'prophet' (*prophetes*) was very familiar to people in Jesus' day because of its prominence in the Old Testament. The prophet was called to proclaim God's Word, and was responsible only to God for the warnings, exhortations, encouragements, and teachings that he gave. John the Baptist was commonly acknowledged as a prophet (Mt. 11:9; 14:5), and some of Jesus' listeners saw him in the same category as well (Mt. 16:13,14; 21:11). But Jesus did not use this term to describe himself, or his followers.

However, very early in the history of the church, people known as prophets were recognized and given leadership in the community. Some of the prophets had an itinerant ministry (Acts 11:27,28; 21:10), as did teachers like Apollos (18:24) and evangelists like Philip (8:5). In other cases, prophets apparently functioned as part of the ongoing leadership of the congregation. For example, prophets and teachers at Antioch commissioned the first missionary team (13:1); Judas and Silas, leaders in the Jerusalem church (15:22), were also known as prophets (15:32); and Paul gave detailed instructions to the Corinthian congregation about the regulation of the prophetic gift in their regular services (1 Cor. 14).

The functions of prophets specifically detailed in the New Testament include warning the Christian community of impending difficulties (Acts 11:28; 21:10,11); speaking to encourage, strengthen, comfort, and instruct believers (Acts 15:32; 1 Cor. 14:3,31); bringing people under personal conviction of sin (1 Cor. 14:24,25); and preparing God's people for works of service (Eph. 4:11,12).

The congregation at Corinth is assumed to have more than one person with the gift of prophecy, for all the prophets are instructed to weigh carefully the messages given by the two or three who are allowed to speak in any given meeting (1 Cor. 14:29–31). The prophets are to speak in an orderly manner and are to acknowledge not only the discipline of the group, but also the authority of Christ's apostles (14:32,33,37,38). Even the most inspired public ministries are designed to serve the needs of the fellowship and are to be expressed within its overall order.

Prophets are often mentioned together with apostles as playing the foundational leadership roles in the church. In 1 Corinthians 12:28, Paul says that God has appointed in the church 'first of all apostles, second prophets'. Similarly, in Ephesians 4:11, he says that Christ gave 'some to be apostles, some to be prophets', and so forth. The church, says Paul in Ephesians 2:20, is 'built on the foundation of the apostles and prophets'. In John's vision, in the chorus of praise over the downfall of Babylon, we find a threefold division of the church: 'Rejoice, saints and apostles and prophets!' (Rev. 18:20).

As with the ministry of the apostle, a distinction should be made between the uniquely authoritative ministry of the first-century prophet in the foundation of the early Christian church, and the broader function of prophetic ministry that continues in the church today. When we say that the church is built on the foundation of the apostles and the prophets, we are referring to a ministry that cannot be duplicated or repeated. The church expresses its continuity with the apostolic tradition through its response to the authority of the canonical Scriptures, which it holds to be complete; it evaluates the teaching and mission of its contemporary leaders in the light of this norm.

R

RACE, OF PEOPLE

In 1 Peter 2:9, Peter describes his readers as a 'chosen people (*genos*)'. The term *genos* is derived from the stem *gen-*, and is related to words like *gennesis* (birth), *gennema* (offspring), and *gennao* (be father of). It emphasizes a line of descent, a lineage. To distinguish it from the word *laos*, which is also translated as 'people', *genos* is best translated as 'race'. Israel was a race chosen from among the other nations (Deut. 7:6; 10:15; Isa. 43:20) to be the arena of God's gracious actions in history, preparing for the birth of the Messiah. Christians have been adopted into this lineage, as spiritual descendants of Abraham, through following his example of faith (Gal. 3:14,29).

REFUSE

In 1 Corinthians 4:13, Paul introduces an image which underscores the suffering and rejection that are an inevitable part of the Christian life. He says, 'Up to this moment we [apostles] have become the scum of the earth, the refuse (*peripsema*) of the world.'

The noun 'refuse' or 'trash' comes from the verb *peripsao* which means to wipe all around, to rub clean, and refers to the scum which is thereby removed. Thus the term vividly connotes rejection, and is well suited for identification with Christ's sufferings as the rejected Messiah.

RESIDENT, TEMPORARY

In his opening greeting to his readers in his first letter, Peter refers to them as 'temporary residents' (*parepidemoi*): 'Peter, an apostle of Jesus Christ, to God's elect, strangers (*parepidemois*) in the world' (1 Pet. 1:1). The word describes someone who lives for a short while in a foreign place as a stranger or alien. It refers to a temporary visitor, a wanderer who has no intention of establishing permanent residence. (See also 'Alien, Resident'.)

RULER, ROYAL

The book of Revelation speaks of believers sharing in Christ's rule as members of his kingdom. The first chapter contains a doxology to Jesus Christ as the one who 'has made us to be a kingdom (*basileian*) and priests to serve his God and Father' (1:6). Chapter five records a song of praise to Jesus, the Lamb, who has purchased, with his own blood, people for God from every corner of the earth. In language similar to that of 1:6, the four living creatures and twenty-four elders sing:

> You have made them to be a kingdom
>> and priests to serve our God,
> and they will reign (*basileusousin*) on the earth (5:10).

Similarly, those who participate with Christ in the first resurrection will reign with him for a thousand years (20:4,6). The servants of God described in Revelation 22:5 are said to reign with him for ever and ever. A related metaphor is the picture of believers sitting on thrones (e.g. 3:21; 20:4; cf. Mt. 19:28; Lk. 22:28–30; Rev. 4:4).

The apostle Paul extends the encouraging promise: 'If we endure, we will also reign with him (*symbasileusomen*)' (2 Tim. 2:12). In the kingdom, all of God's people are destined to rule, to exercise dominion, a destiny far more glorious than even the creation mandate given to human-kind in Genesis 1:28. Jesus promised the disciples that they would sit on thrones judging the twelve tribes of Israel in the coming kingdom (Mt. 19:28; Lk. 22:28–30), but a similar promise is extended to every follower of Jesus as well. Unlike social systems in which some are perpetual rulers and others form a permanent underclass, in the community of the King all share his rule with him.

RUNNER

Twice in 1 Corinthians 9, Paul compares the Christian to a runner: 'Do you not know that in a race all the runners (*trechontes*) run, but only one gets the prize? Run in such a way as to get the prize' (v. 24); also, 'I do not run (*trecho*) like a man running aimlessly' (v. 26). He challenges the Galatians: 'You were running (*etrechete*) a good race. Who cut in on you and kept you from obeying the truth?' (Gal.

5:7). The author of Hebrews urges his readers to 'run (*trechomen*) with endurance' the race marked out for them (12:1).

One of Paul's favourite images for a ministry completed is the image of finishing a race (*dromos*), not dropping out from exhaustion or getting disqualified along the way. In his sermon in the synagogue at Pisidian Antioch, he describes John the Baptist as 'completing his work', literally, 'finishing the race' (Acts 13:25). A few chapters later in Acts, encouraging the Ephesians elders, Paul says that all the sufferings and hardships of his ministry will be worthwhile if only he can 'finish the race' (20:24). Near the end of his life, Paul is finally able to say triumphantly, 'I have finished the race' (2 Tim. 4:7).

S

SAINT

'Saint' (*hagios*) is one of most frequently used terms for followers of Jesus, especially in the writings of Paul[1] and in the book of Revelation.[2] Yet, it is rarely used for members of the holy nation in the Old Testament and is not used at all by Jesus with reference to his disciples. Whenever it is used of Christians in the New Testament, it occurs in the plural. Although God is named 'the Holy One (*tou hagiou*)' (1 Jn. 2:20), as also is Christ (Acts 3:14; Rev. 3:7), no individual Christian is called by this term.

However, the believers are frequently referred to as saints or holy ones (*hagioi*). This term speaks of the special relationship of the believer to God, as one who has been set apart for God's purposes. It reminds us of the distinctive calling, character, privilege, and mission of the Christian.

---

[1] The word occurs more than 35 times in Romans, 1 and 2 Corinthians, Ephesians, Philippians, Colossians, 1 and 2 Thessalonians, 1 Timothy, and Philemon.

[2] At least 12 occurrences.

Sometimes it is used simply as a synonym for 'Christian', as when Luke describes Peter's visit to the 'saints' in Lydda and Joppa (Acts 9:32,41), or when Paul sends greetings to and from the 'saints' (Rom. 16:15; 2 Cor. 13:13; Phil. 4:21,22).

Quite a number of times the word 'saint' is used in connection with ministry, with reference to acts of service and love. For example, Paul refers several times to the offering for the relief of impoverished Christians in Judea as a 'service to the saints' (Rom. 15:25,26,31; 1 Cor. 16:1; 2 Cor. 8:2; 9:1,12). He frequently commends those who have loved, helped, served, or refreshed the 'saints' (1 Cor. 16:15; Eph. 1:15; Colossians 1:14; 1 Tim. 5:10; Phil. 5:6). In Ephesians 4 he describes how gifted individuals have been supplied to the church by Christ 'to prepare God's people [i.e. 'the saints', *ton hagion*] for works of service' (v. 12). Perhaps this word is used to express the special importance of these people to God, and therefore their value and worth as both recipients of ministry and agents of ministry.

Several other passages speak of the marvellous privileges that are available to the saints. They are called by God (Rom. 1:7; 1 Cor. 1:20). The Spirit intercedes for them (Rom. 8:27). They will judge the world (1 Cor. 6:1,2). They will receive a glorious inheritance (Eph. 1:18; Col. 1:12). The privileges of citizenship are theirs (Eph. 2:19). They experience the love of God (Eph. 3:18). Mysteries are disclosed to them (Col. 1:26). They have been promised future glorification (2 Thess. 1:10). The matchless faith of the gospel has been entrusted to them (Jude 3).

Yet none of these benefits exempt the saints from suffering. Many of the references in the book of Revelation are to the suffering and warfare of the saints (12:7,10; 14:12; 16:6; 17:6; 18:24). Nevertheless, their prayers are heard by

God (5:8; 8:3,4) and their final triumph is assured (11:18; 18:20). To be a saint means ultimately to be rescued and rewarded by God, but not to be shielded from all pain and conflict in the meantime.

In only a few cases is the term 'saint' specifically associated with the call to holy living. In Ephesians 5:3 Paul urges Christians to avoid sexual immorality, impurity, and greed, because 'these are improper for God's holy people (*hagiois*)'. In Revelation 19:8, the bride of the Lamb is dressed in bright, clean, fine linen, representing 'the righteous acts of the saints'.

SALT

One of the best-known metaphors used by Jesus to describe his disciples occurs in the Sermon on the Mount, where he says, 'You are the salt (*halas*) of the earth' (Mt. 5:13). Many have offered explanations of the significance of salt in the society of that time, but the two aspects of salt that appear most prominently are enhancement of flavour and preservation from decay. Thus, through this illustration, Jesus is highlighting the distinctive identity of his disciples as those who display God's character before the world and who help to rescue people from the judgement to come.

The image of salt implies that the disciples are going to influence their society. It summons them to the task of penetration and renewal. The followers of Jesus will have an observable impact on their world, not so much through their actions as through their very character as salt.

Yet, Jesus warns, it is possible for salt to lose its saltiness, and hence to become ineffective and useless, good for nothing except to be thrown out and trampled. The danger of salt losing its distinctive character is also mentioned by Jesus in Luke 14:34,35: 'Salt is good, but if it loses its saltiness, how can it be made salty again? It is fit neither for the soil nor for the manure heap; it is thrown out' (cf. Mk. 9:50).

SCUM

In 1 Corinthians 4:13, Paul says, 'Up to this moment we [apostles] have become the scum (*perikatharmata*) of the earth, the refuse of the world.' The word translated 'scum' is compounded from the verb *kathairo* ('to make clean') and the preposition *peri* ('around'). It describes the result of a very thorough scouring, that is, the dirt that is removed through intense scrubbing. Those who voluntarily sacrifice their lives for the sake of Christ are not understood by the world; they are viewed with contempt by those who see life's goals only in terms of the achievement of honours or possessions.

SEAL

The term 'seal' (*sphragis*) refers to the signet ring itself, the gemstone set in the ring, the engraving on the stone, and the imprint made by the signet ring. The seal was used to mark personal property, to symbolize authority, and to serve as a guarantee or sign of protection.

Paul says to the Corinthians that he should not have to defend his position as a true apostle of Christ, because, 'you are the seal of my apostleship in the Lord' (1 Cor. 9:2). Here the seal is used as a symbol of the genuine article; the

Corinthians are the proof that Paul is not an impostor; their spiritual life and existence as a community testify to the integrity and effectiveness of Paul's apostolic work in preaching the gospel and establishing churches.

SEED / WHEAT

After presenting the parable of the wheat and the weeds (Mt. 13:24–30, 36–43), Jesus explains to his disciples that 'the good seed (*sperma*) stands for the sons of the kingdom' (13:38). The Son of Man sows these seeds in the field, which represents the world, where the good seed grows alongside the weeds sown by the devil. Not until the end of the age can the two be separated. At that time, says Jesus, the wheat (*siton*), grown from the good seed, will be harvested and gathered into the barn, while the weeds will be tied in bundles and burned.

The point of the parable is that the weeds and the wheat cannot be separated until the end of the age. In attempting to uproot the one, you would destroy the other. Thus the disciples are called to live alongside unbelievers in the world. They are not to attempt to withdraw into isolated communities, but are to live among the people of the world, trusting that at last they will be vindicated and revealed as the objects of God's special protection and choice.

The metaphor of the seed occurs again in John 12:24, where Jesus speaks of the imminent approach of his time of suffering. He compares the disciple to the kernel of wheat which must fall to the ground and die before it can produce many other seeds. As in the images of the soil and the vine, the emphasis is on fruitfulness. The goal or purpose of the seed is to produce more seeds. The disciple who refuses to pay the costs necessary for fruitfulness proves himself to be no true servant of Jesus. Here the image of the seed implies sacrifice, and participation in the sufferings of Christ, in order to accomplish the mission.

SERVANT

Several different Greek words are translated by the same English word 'servant'. The two words used most frequently by Jesus to express the idea of servanthood are *diakonos* and *doulos*. Because they frequently occur together in the same passages, it is difficult to distinguish the two words. One pattern that emerges is that when the emphasis is on the task, the responsibility, on obeying orders and being under authority, the word used is *doulos*. But when the emphasis is on the rendering of personal service, or on the attitudes of humility and love which should inspire the service, then the word more likely to be used is *diakonos*.

Diakonos

The verb *diakonein* on which the noun *diakonos* is based means literally 'to wait at table', to render service during a meal. This sense is found in Jesus' parable in Luke 17:8 where the servant is commanded by his master to prepare the supper and to serve it, and also in the surprising description in Luke 12:37 of the master who turns the tables and thanks the faithful servants by waiting on them himself!

The image of the *diakonos* is often connected with Jesus' teachings on humility. For example, Mark refers to an argument between the disciples on the road to Capernaum about who was the greatest (a topic that came up frequently among the twelve). The disciples were embarrassed to tell Jesus what they had been discussing. So Jesus called them together and sat down, as a symbol of his own authority. Then he said: 'If anyone wants to be first, he must be the very last, and the servant (*diakonos*) of all' (Mk. 9:35). The servant of *all* would make no distinctions concerning whom he would serve and whom he would not. Such servanthood is an unqualified act of surrender to be available to anyone to whom the master sends us.

Then Jesus used a child as an illustration of the kind of humble attitude God was looking for. The parallel account in Matthew records Jesus' statement: 'Whoever humbles himself like this child is the greatest in the kingdom of heaven' (Mt. 18:4). Luke's account includes the statement: 'He who is least among you all – he is the greatest' (Lk. 9:48).

A similar dispute broke out when James and John requested positions of honour at the right and left hands of Jesus (Mt. 20:20–28 and Mk. 10:35–45). Jesus replied by pointing out the contrast between the harsh and arrogant rule of the Gentile authorities, and the humble servanthood to which he was calling his disciples. He said, 'Whoever wants to become great among you must be your servant (*diakonos*)' (Mt. 20:26), then concluded with the citation of his own example: 'For even the Son of Man did not come to be served (*diakonethenai*), but to serve (*diakonesai*), and to give his life as a ransom for many' (Mk. 10:45).

Luke 22 records yet a third argument on the same topic, following the Last Supper. As in Matthew 20, Jesus contrasts the practices of Gentile rulers with the standards expected of his followers. He says:

The kings of the Gentiles lord it over them; and those who exercise authority over them call themselves Benefactors. But you are not to be like that. Instead, the greatest among you should be like the youngest, and the one who rules like the one who serves (*diakonon*). For who is greater, the one who is at the table or the one who serves (*diakonon*)? Is it not the one who is at the table? But I am among you as one who serves (*diakonon*). (Lk. 20:25–27)

In that Jesus had just finished washing the disciples' feet, the illustration of his service to them was fresh in their minds. Jesus was not rebuking the desire to be great, or denying that there could be authority or rule within his community. Rather, he was teaching that the attitude underlying every action was to be that of the humble servant.

Matthew records yet another example of the association between the word *diakonos* and the attitude of humility. In the midst of a scathing denunciation of the Pharisees for their hypocrisy, their preoccupation with outward appearance, and their clamouring for recognition, Jesus says: 'The greatest among you will be your servant (*diakonos*). For whoever exalts himself will be humbled, and whoever humbles himself will be exalted' (23:11,12).

The greatest act of humility and self-emptying servanthood by far is seen in Jesus' giving of his life 'as a ransom for many' (Mt. 20:28; Mk. 10:45). The word *diakonos* is used once more by Jesus in John 12, in association with his imminent death. He tells a short parable about the kernel of wheat which must fall into the ground and die in order to become fruitful (12:24). He reminds the disciples that, 'The man who loves his life will lose it, while the man who hates his life in this world will keep it for eternal life' (12:25). And then he says:

> Whoever serves (*diakonei*) me must follow me; and where I
> am, my servant (*diakonos*) also will be. My Father will honour
> the one who serves (*diakonei*) me (12:26).

Thus to serve Jesus is to follow him, to stay with him no
matter where the path may lead, even to suffering and
death.

In the New Testament as a whole, the most common
set of terms for service are the cluster consisting of *diakonos*
(servant), *diakonia* (service), and *diakoneo* (to serve). The
verb is used for the ministry of all Christians in 1 Peter 4:10:
'Each one should use whatever gift he has received to serve
others'. The noun 'service' (*diakonia*) is applied to quite a
variety of different ministries in the New Testament, including the role of apostle within the circle of the twelve
(Acts 1:25) as well as Paul's apostolic calling (Acts 20:24;
1 Tim. 1:12), the new covenant ministry exercised by Paul
and Timothy (2 Cor. 4:1), the offering collected for impoverished Christians in Judea (2 Cor. 8:4; 9:1,12,13), and
the ministry of the whole church (Eph. 4:12). In Acts 6,
both the administration of the funds for the widows (v. 1),
and the apostles' work in the Word and prayer (v. 4), are
referred to as 'ministry' or 'service' (*diakonia*).

So, then, the word *diakonia* is quite general and com-
prehensive. It includes apostolic leadership, proclamation
of the gospel, relief of the needs of the poor, and the
individual ministries of all the members of the church. Both
the highest responsibilities of leadership and the most
humble forms of helpfulness are included under the term
'service'. The ground is level for all. No function is so
exalted that it ceases to be essentially 'service', nor is any
task so small or lowly that it cannot be dignified by the same
term.

As we have already noted, the basic meaning of *diakonos* is one who serves at table. It becomes one of Paul's favourite terms for describing himself and his co-workers. The individuals who are identified as *diakonos* or *syndouolos* ('fellow servant') by Paul include Phoebe (Rom. 16:1), Tychicus (Eph. 6:21; Col. 4:7), Epaphras (Col. 1:7), Timothy (included in the 'we' of 2 Corinthians 3:6 and 6:4), and Apollos (1 Cor. 3:5). Paul designates himself as a servant of Christ in 2 Corinthians 11:23, as a servant of the gospel in Colossians 1:23, and as a servant of the church in Colossians 1:25.

It is interesting to observe how Paul employs this word *diakonos* when his ministry is under attack, or when he is being compared unfavourably to other leaders. Instead of insisting on his superiority to Apollos, he reminds the Corinthians that even the greatest leaders are no more than 'servants (*diakonoi*), through whom you came to believe – as the Lord has assigned to each his task' (1 Cor. 3:5). He defends the integrity of his ministry by pointing to the sufferings which he has gladly endured as a 'servant of God' (2 Cor. 6:3–11) and 'servant of Christ' (2 Cor. 11:23–33). In the same spirit of humility in Ephesians 3, after calling himself a 'servant of the gospel' (v. 7), Paul says that he is 'less than the least of all God's people' (v. 8). In Colossians 1, he links his role as 'servant of the church' with participation in Christ's sufferings (vv. 24,25).

Thus the term *diakonos* may be used to describe a church leader, but the emphasis is on humility and on helpfulness, not on authority or status. New Testament leadership begins with the recognition that even the leader with the greatest responsibilities is no more than a humble table waiter, expected to endure suffering as part of the call to service in Christ's name. This leadership means service to Christ, to the gospel, and to the church – there is no place for personal aggrandizement or kingdom-building.

On two occasions Paul uses *diakonos* to describe a specific group of individuals within the church. He addresses his letter to the Philippians: 'To all the saints in Christ Jesus at Philippi, together with the overseers and deacons (*diakonois*)' (1:1). Here the deacons are plainly leaders of the church, engaged in particular areas of service, perhaps like the seven who were appointed in Acts 6 (even though the seven are never actually called 'deacons'). In 1 Timothy 3, after defining the qualifications for overseers, Paul lists the requirements for the 'deacon' (*diakonos*), which include the same standards of exemplary life, but do not include the requirement of teaching skill.[3]

The specific responsibilities of the deacons are not spelled out in the New Testament, perhaps because the office was still relatively new, or perhaps because the structure was intended to be fluid, adaptable to changing needs and local circumstances. That is, each congregation, as it grew large enough, might appoint individuals to administer certain areas, but there was nothing fixed about the position or the responsibility. It was basically a function established in response to a particular need, rather than a permanent office. It focused and organized the ministry of service that was still the task of every believer and every leader.

---

[3] It is not clear whether the reference to *gynaikas* in 1 Timothy 3:11 means the wives of the deacons, or women who function as deaconesses. Nor is it certain whether Phoebe (Acts 16:1) held an official position as deaconess in the church at Cenchrea, or whether Paul was using *diakonos* in the more general sense, commending her as one who engaged in acts of service, as he does with Tychicus and Epaphras.

Doulos

The other word translated 'servant' used most often by Jesus is *doulos*. This is the most general word for servant or slave, and is related to the words *syndoulos* (fellow-servant), *douleuo* (to serve) and *douloo* (to make someone a slave). The word group has a strong emphasis on being under the authority of another – most often, the authority of God.

When Jesus speaks to his disciples of servanthood, he has two aspects in mind. First is the service rendered to *God* as the supreme authority to whom they owe their allegiance, and the second is the service which they render to *people* as an expression of humility and love.

In the Sermon on the Mount, Jesus warns his disciples:

> No-one can serve (*douleuein*) two masters. Either he will hate the one and love the other, or he will be devoted to the one and despise the other. You cannot serve (*douleuein*) both God and Money (Mt. 6:24; cf. Lk. 16:13).

The relationship of service involves obedience, but it is more than that – it is also a matter of allegiance. The conflict that Jesus describes is not a conflict in chains of command, but rather a matter of divided affections. The key words are love and devotion, in contrast to hating and despising. Thus, says Jesus, the service that God requires springs from an exclusive allegiance.

Many times in his parables Jesus compares his followers to servants (*douloi*), whether of a king, or head of a household, or landowner. For example, in the parable of the unforgiving servant (Mt. 18:23–35), a servant who has been forgiven a huge debt by the king refuses to release his fellow-servant (*syndoulon*) from a much smaller obligation.

In the parable of the prodigal son, the older son complains about all the years he has served his father without special recognition (Lk. 15:29).

In the parable of the talents (Mt. 25:14–30), a man entrusts various large sums of money to his servants, expecting them to invest the resources wisely during his absence. The huge amounts of money involved illustrate the significant level of responsibility that the Lord entrusts to his servants. The strong reaction of the master to the servant who fails to exercise stewardship shows the great importance Jesus places on the disciples' diligence in using effectively the resources they have been given for the task of ministry.

In a similar story, the parable of the ten minas (Lk. 19:12–27), the amounts of money are much smaller, and the emphasis is on the long delay that will precede the coming of the kingdom. The story stresses the importance of making the most of opportunities in the meantime. The faithful servants are rewarded by being given authority over several cities. They are not released from their continuing obligation to serve, but they gain the privilege of broadened responsibility. Both parables teach that servanthood involves responsibility and accountability, and that faithful service will be rewarded.

The association of servanthood with responsibility is also found in Jesus' comments in Matthew 24:45–51 (cf. Lk. 12:42–46) about the 'faithful and wise servant (*doulos*)' whom the master puts in charge of his other household servants (*oiketeias*) to give them their food at the proper time. This servant has other servants under him. And he is rewarded by being placed in charge of all his master's possessions (24:47). In contrast, the wicked servant is described as mistreating his fellow-servants (*syndoulous*). Thus even though this servant has responsibility over others, he still remains a servant – not just 'over', but also 'among'. Luke follows his telling of this story with Jesus' warning to the servant who has been entrusted with much, but who does not obey (Lk. 12:47,48).

Similarly, in Mark 13:34, during the Olivet discourse, Jesus speaks about a person who leaves his house and places his servants (*doulois*) in charge, each with his own task. Each servant is given authority over a particular area.

In Luke 12:35–38, Jesus paints a beautiful portrait of the high regard which the master has for his faithful servants. He pictures a man returning from a wedding banquet to find his servants waiting for him. Jesus says, 'I tell you the truth, he will dress himself to serve, will have them recline at the table and will come and wait on them.' What a startling and unexpected expression of the master's approval!

The standard of service that God expects is revealed vividly in Luke 17. Jesus has just told the disciples that they must be prepared to forgive again and again the brother who sins against them repeatedly. Apparently overwhelmed by these high standards, the disciples cry out, 'Increase our faith!' (17:5). Jesus speaks of the power of faith as small as a mustard seed, but then goes on to raise the standard even higher. He describes a servant (*doulos*) who has been ploughing or looking after the sheep. After the servant finishes his work in the fields he is expected to prepare supper for the master and to wait on his needs. Only then can he prepare his own meal. And in all of these tasks he is not to expect any special thanks from the master, because he is merely performing his duty. Thus Jesus concludes: 'So you also, when you have done everything you were told to do, should say, "We are unworthy servants; we have only done our duty" ' (17:10). When the disciples keep the commands of Jesus, they are not to congratulate themselves on their extraordinary accomplishment, or to expect special recognition; they are only doing their duty; the same would be expected of any servant. The truly valuable servant will find ways to serve that go beyond the mere commands of the master; he will delight to identify needs of the master, and to fulfill them before he is even asked to do so. The true servant has his master's welfare on his heart at all times.

To be Jesus' servant is to be identified closely with him in all respects, including his suffering. In Matthew 10, Jesus warns the disciples about the persecution which they are going to suffer because of their association with him, telling them that they must not expect any better treatment than he himself has received. He says:

> A student is not above his teacher, nor a servant (*doulos*) above his master. It is enough for the student to be like his teacher, and the servant (*doulos*) like his master (10:24,25).

Jesus makes a similar statement ('a servant is not greater than his master') in a similar context (a warning about persecution) in John 15:20. Then again, in John 13:16 we find the same quotation, when Jesus exhorts the disciples to wash one another's feet, and not to consider beneath their dignity the sort of humble work that their Master was willing to do.

Although Jesus used the metaphor of the servant frequently in reference to his disciples, he saw its limitations. Although the 'servant' image conveyed the ideas of accomplishing a task, fulfilling a responsibility, and being under authority, it could not express the quality of intimate relationship that Jesus enjoyed with his disciples. Thus he said to his disciples in John 15:15: 'I no longer call you servants (*doulous*), because a servant does not know his master's business. Instead, I have called you friends, for everything that I learned from my Father I have made known to you.' When Jesus said 'no longer', he reminded them of what a dominant metaphor 'servant' had been in his teaching so far.

Yet to be a servant implies not only allegiance to the Lord. It also involves an attitude of humility toward others. In Matthew 20:20–28 (cf. Mk. 10:35–45) we find James and John making the request, through their mother, to be given the two positions of greatest prominence in the kingdom – sitting at Jesus' right and left. Jesus has just told the disciples that he is going up to Jerusalem to suffer and to die (Mt. 20:17–19), but they do not grasp the implications. Anger erupts from the ten toward the presumption of the two, probably out of jealousy that the others did not think to make the request first!

Jesus corrects their attitudes by drawing a contrast between leadership in pagan society and leadership in his community: 'You know that the rulers of the Gentiles lord it over them, and their high officials exercise authority over them' (Mt. 20:25). The phrases 'lord it over' and 'exercise authority' express looking *down*, subjugation, oppression, abuse of power and authority. But that is not to be the case with the twelve. Jesus says, 'Whoever wants to become great among you must be your servant (*diakonos*), and whoever wants to be first must be your slave (*doulos*)' (20:26,27). Then Jesus cites his own example of service, in contrast to the typical patterns of the world: '. . . just as the Son of Man did not come to be served, but to serve, and to give his life as a ransom for many' (20:28).

Notice that here Jesus does not call the disciples to be servants in a general sense. No, he exhorts them specifically to be servants of *one another*. That is much more difficult. To serve their master is expected. But to serve their *competitors* is far more challenging. They are to be so busy lifting one another up that they forget about their own ambitions, and instead become caught up in the joy of seeing one another succeed. Instead of focusing on being *over*, they are to place themselves willingly *under*, and in so doing, they will become great. Thus the image of 'servant' expresses humility, and the willing withdrawal from the competition for status and power.

There were a good number of slaves in the early churches, but these were exhorted to serve their masters as if they were serving the Lord (Eph. 6:6,7; Col. 3:2,3). Even menial work took on a new dignity and found a new and higher standard of excellence when seen as service offered to Christ himself.

But the term *doulos* was also applied figuratively to the whole community of believers, no matter what their social status. Peter urged all his readers to 'live as servants (*douloi*) of God' (1 Pet. 2:16). Throughout the book of Revelation, John referred to believers as servants (*douloi*) and fellow-servants (*syndouloi*) of God (1:1; 2:20; 6:11; 7:4; 19:2,5; 22:3,6). Paul commended the Thessalonians for turning from idols 'to serve (*douleuein*) the living and true God' (1 Thess. 1:9); this phrase summarizes the whole intent and purpose of the Christian life.

In particular, the leaders of the early church gladly applied this term to themselves. Paul introduces himself to the Romans as 'a servant of Jesus Christ' (1:1); in Galatians 1:10 he says that if he were still trying to please men he would not be a 'servant of Christ'; in writing to Titus, he calls himself a 'servant of God' (1:1). In their salutation to the Philippians, Paul and Timothy refer to themselves as 'servants of Christ' (1:1). Similarly, James calls himself a 'servant of God' (1:1), Peter introduces himself as a 'servant and apostle of Jesus Christ' (2 Pet. 1:1), and Jude identifies himself as a 'servant of Jesus Christ' (v. 1).

Paul expresses thankfulness for Timothy as one who served (*edouleusen*) with him in the work of the gospel, like a son serving with his father (Phil. 2:22). He also commends Epaphras as 'our dear fellow-servant (*syndoulou*)' (Col. 1:7), and as a 'servant of Jesus Christ' (Col. 4:12). He refers to Tychicus as a 'fellow-servant in the Lord' (Col. 4:7). When writing to Timothy, Paul reminds him that 'the Lord's servant must not quarrel' (2 Tim. 2:24). Thus both apostles and their co-workers are described as 'servants' (*douloi*). Those in the highest positions of leadership do not hesitate to picture themselves in the lowest status of servanthood, following the Master, who said, 'Whoever wants to be first must be your slave (*doulos*)' (Mt. 20:27).

The apostle Paul spoke of himself not only as a servant (*doulos*) of the Lord Jesus, but also of the Lord's people. Both times he used this image it was in writing to a proud, self-centred church, preoccupied with matters of status and fractured with competition and rude behaviour. To them Paul wrote about his willingness to forfeit his rights, and his desire to 'make [himself] a slave (*edoulosa*) to everyone', (2 Cor. 9:19) to bring more people to Christ. In his second letter to the Corinthians he says even more directly, 'We do not preach ourselves, but Jesus Christ as Lord, and ourselves as your servants (*doulous*) for Jesus' sake' (2 Cor. 4:5). Paul's ultimate accountability is still to Christ; but Christ has assigned him the task of serving the

Corinthians, as the master of a household assigns certain slaves to attend to the honoured guests.

For us who live in a society where slavery as a social institution has long since been abolished, it is difficult to appreciate how startling this imagery must have been to people in the Hellenistic world. The Romans had more slaves than any previous society. During the relatively peaceful years in which the New Testament was written, the slave trade was less active, and the majority of slaves were born and raised in captivity. Slaves worked in all sorts of circumstances – in miserable conditions in the fields and in the mines, and sometimes in relative comfort as managers of households, as physicians, or as educators. Yet in spite of the widespread acceptance of the practice, and the relatively humane conditions in which many household slaves lived, slavery was viewed by the Greeks and the Romans as a despicable condition.

Yet slavery was the image that became the dominant metaphor for Christian service and leadership. More than anything, it emphasized that the Christian did not belong to himself or herself. The follower of Jesus was under authority, obligated to go where he commanded, to do the tasks that he assigned, to serve whenever the Master spoke and whomever the Master wished.

A number of other words related to servanthood highlight various aspects of the task to which the servant of the Lord may be assigned. The word *hyperetes* (servant) is used by Jesus of his disciples in just one passage. In his examination before Pilate, Jesus is asked, 'Are you the king of the Jews?' (Jn. 18:33). And after a brief interchange Jesus says, 'My kingdom is not of this world. If it were, my servants (*hyperetai*) would fight to prevent my arrest by the Jews' (Jn. 18:36).

In the gospels, the word *hyperetes* is generally used to describe the officers who aid those in positions of leadership such as judges and chief priests. For example, in Matthew 5:25 Jesus urges his disciples to settle disputes quickly with their adversaries, so that they are not handed over to the judge, who may in turn hand them over to the officer (*hyperete*) who will throw them in prison. Throughout the gospel of John the word is used to describe the officers sent by the chief priests and Pharisees to place Jesus under arrest (7:32; 18:3,12,18,22; 19:6).[4]

In these contexts the *hyperetes* had as his main function the carrying out of the orders of another. He is one who helps, who assists in the task. His role is defined with reference to the one he serves. In using this metaphor of his disciples, Jesus was indicating that their function was to assist him in his ministry and to carry out his commands.

The word *hyperetes* is applied literally to John Mark in Acts 13, where he accompanies Barnabas and Saul as their 'helper'. Originally *hyperetes* referred to a rower, a galley slave, one of the most miserable and difficult tasks that could be assigned. Paul says that this term was first applied to him by the Lord himself. When recounting the story of his conversion before Agrippa, Bernice, and Festus, Paul tells how the risen Lord Jesus met him on the Damascus road, and commissioned him: 'I have appeared to you to appoint you as a servant (*hypereten*) and as a witness of what you have seen of me and what I will show you' (Acts 26:16). In speaking of the roles that he, Apollos, and Cephas play in the church, Paul employs the same metaphor, saying, 'So, then, men ought to regard us as servants (*hyperetas*) of Christ and as those entrusted (*oikonomous*) with the secret

---

[4] The word is also used in Luke 4:20 of the synagogue attendant.

things of God' (1 Cor. 4:1). In this verse Paul combines two servant words from opposite ends of the spectrum – the lowly galley slave (*hyperetes*) on the one hand, and the household manager or steward (*oikonomos*) on the other. Yes, he and the other apostles have been given great responsibility by the Lord, but in essence they remain nothing more than humble servants of the one who assigned them the task.

Another word for servant used by Jesus was *oiketes*. Following the parable of the shrewd manager, Jesus says to his disciples:

> No servant (*oiketes*) can serve (*douleuein*) two masters. Either he will hate the one and love the other, or he will be devoted to the one and despise the other. You cannot serve both God and Money (Lk. 16:13).

The *oiketes* is a kind of servant named for his sphere of service – that is, within the household (*oikos*), in contrast to servants who work in the fields, or who manage business interests, or who assist the chief priests. Like other kinds of servants, he is under the authority of a master, and shares the function of serving expressed by the verb *douleuein*. In the use of this metaphor, Jesus reminds the disciples that they can have only one ultimate authority for their lives, but also that they are members of God's household.

Paul refers to the household servant (*oiketes*) in Romans 14:4, in his discussion of differing attitudes toward doubtful practices. He asks, 'Who are you to judge someone else's servant (*oiketen*)? To his own master he stands or falls.' To be a servant of the Lord, then, is to have a clear line of accountability to him that frees us from bending to every opinion of others who would evaluate us. To call a fellow believer a servant of the Lord is likewise to give that one the freedom to follow the dictates of his or her own conscience.

Yet another 'servant' word is employed by Jesus in Luke 12:42, where he asks, 'Who then is the faithful and wise manager, whom the master puts in charge of his servants (*therapeias*) to give them their food allowance at the proper time?' A few verses later these servants are referred to as menservants (*paidas*) and womenservants (*paidiskas*) (12:45). In the parallel passage found in Matthew 24:45, the noun *oiketeias* ('domestic servants') is substituted for *therapeias*.

From other usages of the noun *therapeia* and the related verb *therapeuo*, it appears that the emphasis of the word group is on personal care. Thus the *therapeia* as servant is one who waits upon the master, rendering personal assistance.

The remaining two servant terms are not used by Jesus in the gospels, but rather are introduced by Paul in his letters. The first is not a noun, but since it is sometimes translated as 'serve', it is included here. The verb *latreuo* (to serve) refers to the service of God by the whole people and by the individual worshipper, whether in formal acts of worship or in the personal adoration of the heart. In Romans 1:9, Paul speaks of 'God, whom I serve (*latreuo*) with my whole heart'. Then in Romans 12:1, where he urges his readers to offer their bodies as living sacrifices, as their 'spiritual [act of] worship (*latreian*)', Paul uses the same imagery to describe every Christian's service to God. Paul uses the verb *latreuo* again in 2 Timothy 1:3, where he says, 'I thank God, whom I serve, as my forefathers did . . .'

Paul is not the only New Testament writer to use this term for Christian service. In Revelation 7:15 the white-robed multitude from every nation, tribe, people, and language, are said to be before the throne of God to 'serve him day and night in his temple'. Later, in his vision of the new Jerusalem, John pictures the throne of God and of the Lamb, saying, 'his servants (*douloi*) will serve (*latreusousin*) him' (22:3). Here then is an image of service which will continue to be appropriate into all eternity, even after all earthly tasks are accomplished, and when service on the human level may no longer be necessary or even possible.

The closely related term *leitourgeo*, also translated as 'serve', along with the related noun *leitourgos* ('servant'), has a broader frame of reference. In classical Greek, *leitourgeo* means to do public work at one's own expense, but from the narrow political sense it broadens to refer to almost any type of service. In the Old Testament, *leitourgeo* is used exclusively for the service of priests, unlike *latreuo*, which can also refer to the service of people in general. The word *leitourgos* ('servant') is applied to government officials in Romans 13:6, and to Epaphroditus in his role of rendering help to the apostle Paul in Philippians 2:25,30. In neither case is the image used in a religious sense. However, in Romans 15:16, Paul thanks God for the grace given to him to be:

> . . . a minister (*leitourgon*) of Christ Jesus to the Gentiles with the priestly duty of proclaiming the gospel of God, so that the Gentiles might become an offering acceptable to God, sanctified by the Holy Spirit.

The combination of all of these metaphors related to priestly service plainly show that here *leitourgos* ('servant', 'minister') is not being used in the broader sense of 'public servant', but rather of service in public worship.

SHEEP (see also FLOCK)

One of the metaphors that Jesus uses frequently to describe his followers is that of 'sheep' (*probaton*), as well the related words translated 'flock' (*poimne* and *poimnion*). In Matthew 10, when Jesus sends out the twelve, he warns them: 'I am sending you out like sheep among wolves' (Mt. 10:16). This is a picture of helplessness, of vulnerability. The disciples must rely on God, for as sheep they have no natural defences.

In Matthew 26:31, as well as in the parallel in Mark 14:27, once again the vulnerability of the sheep is in focus. Following the Last Supper, Jesus leads his disciples out onto the Mount of Olives. There he sadly predicts that all of them will fall away and desert him. He quotes these words from the prophet Zechariah: 'I will strike the shepherd, and the sheep of the flock will be scattered.' Here the emphasis is on the dispersion of the sheep that happens so quickly when the shepherd is removed. Sheep do not naturally stay together without a shepherd.

In Luke 12 Jesus tells his disciples not to worry about the physical necessities of life, such as food or clothing, because God knows their needs, and will provide for those who seek first his kingdom. He reassures them, 'Do not be afraid, little flock (*poimnion*), for your Father has been pleased to give you the kingdom' (12:32). The image again is one of helplessness. But the Father has committed himself to see that the needs of the sheep are provided. The shepherd guarantees the sheep's security.

In the familiar parable of the sheep and the goats (Mt. 25:31–46), the sheep are placed to the king's right and the goats to his left. The sheep are identified as those blessed by the Father (25:34), the 'righteous' (25:37,46) who have shown kindness to the brothers of the King. The focus of the parable, however, is on the separation which the King performs, like a shepherd (25:32), and not on the characteristics of sheep.

In John 10 Jesus introduces an extended description of himself as the Good Shepherd. Although the emphasis of the passage is on the self-sacrificing love of the shepherd, there are also many comments about the sheep. The sheep are called by name (10:3) and know the shepherd's voice (10:4,27); that is, they have a personal relationship with the shepherd. The disciples are not anonymous faces among the crowd. The sheep know the shepherd just as the shepherd knows the sheep (10:14,15,27). The sheep are led out by the shepherd (10:3); they follow him (10:4,27); they are dependent on the shepherd for guidance. Thus disciples do not take their own initiative or choose their own paths. The sheep owe their very lives to the shepherd and to his willingness to lay down his life for theirs (10:11); they are fully secure in his care (10:28,29).

Thus, in John 10 the metaphor of the sheep conveys ideas of intimacy, dependence, obedience, and security. But there is another dimension suggested in verse 16, where Jesus says that there remain some sheep who are yet to be gathered into the flock. Here there are hints of evangelism and outreach, leading to the growth of the flock. This is the activity of the shepherd, not the sheep, it is true, but Jesus' statement implants an expectation among the sheep that they must be prepared to welcome others into their circle.

The same terms for 'sheep' and 'flock' are used, with similar associations, by the other New Testament writers. In the two passages where the word 'sheep' (*probaton*) is used, the focus is on Christians under the shepherding care of Jesus. The author of Hebrews refers to Jesus as the 'Great Shepherd of the sheep' (13:20). Peter focuses on the tendency of sheep to wander, and reminds his readers: 'You were like sheep going astray, but now you have returned to the Shepherd and Overseer of your souls' (1 Pet. 2:25).

In the passages which speak of the 'flock' (*poimnion*), however, the references to shepherds point to human leaders of the congregation. In Acts 20:28,29, Paul urges the Ephesian elders to keep watch over 'all the flock', and to guard against the savage wolves that 'will not spare the flock'. In his first letter, likewise addressing elders, Peter urges them to 'be shepherds of God's flock', and to be 'examples to the flock' (1 Pet. 5:2,3). The first passage speaks of the sheep's need for protection; the second focuses on their need for instruction in right behaviour.

The image of the 'flock' also underscores the corporate nature of the Christian life. The shepherd attends to the needs of the individual sheep, but also deals with them as a group, leading them to pasture and protecting them from marauders.

SHEPHERD

Generally in the gospels the shepherd metaphor is applied to Jesus, not to the disciples (cf. Mt. 26:31; Lk. 15:3–7; Jn. 10:11). The disciples are most often described as sheep, not as shepherds. On one occasion, after the resurrection, Jesus instructs a disciple explicitly to do the work of a shepherd. Yet even here the noun 'shepherd' (*poimen*) is not used, but rather two related verbs.

The passage is John 21. Following the miraculous catch of fish, and breakfast together on the shore, Jesus asks Peter the first of three penetrating questions that correspond to Peter's threefold denial. 'Simon son of John, do you truly love me more than these?' When Peter answers, 'Yes, Lord, you know that I love you', Jesus replies, 'Feed (*boske*) my lambs (*arnia*)' (21:15). A second time Jesus poses the question, Peter affirms his love, and Jesus responds with a command: 'Take care of (*poimaine*) my sheep (*probata*)' (21:16). Then comes Jesus' third question, Peter's repeated protest of love, and Jesus' third admonition: 'Feed (*boske*) my sheep (*probata*)' (21:17).

Three times Jesus tells Peter to do the work of a shepherd. Jesus includes the more general word for tending a flock (*poimaine*) in between uses of the more specific word for feeding and pasturing (*boske*). He begins by pointing to those who are the younger, more tender sheep, those most in need of care – the lambs; but he exhorts Peter to care for the whole flock as well. Peter's obedience in taking up the task of shepherding will be the evidence of his genuine love for Jesus.

Notice that Jesus refers all three times to '*my* lambs', '*my* sheep'. The sheep belong to Jesus, not to Peter. The disciple, even as shepherd, remains a servant, caring for the property of another. The emphasis is not on the authority of the shepherd, or the leadership of the shepherd, but on the loving care rendered by the shepherd, and on the accountability of the shepherd to the owner of the sheep. As used by Jesus in this context, the shepherd is a very tender, personal, care-oriented image, though in other passages the verb 'to shepherd' (*poimaino*) can convey a strong sense of authority and rule (cf. Rev. 2:27; 12:5; 19:15).

Although these verses in John are the only ones where a follower of Jesus is described explicitly in shepherding imagery, the shepherding role of the disciples is hinted at in one other place. In Matthew 10:6, Jesus sends the twelve to 'the lost sheep of Israel'. Thus he implies that the disciples will participate in the shepherd's work of gathering the flock.

After the ascension, when Jesus was no longer present to give personal leadership to his flock, the shepherd metaphor became more prominent in the Christian community. Paul exhorts the elders of the Ephesian church in Acts 20:28: 'Be shepherds (*poimainein*) of the church of God, which he bought with his own blood.' The function of shepherding which Paul emphasizes in this passage is that of guarding the flock from the 'savage wolves', the false teachers who will try to come in and draw away disciples. In his first letter, also speaking to elders, Peter says: 'Be shepherds (*poimanate*) of God's flock that is under your care' (5:2). In both cases, the flock belongs to God, not to the shepherd. The shepherd is a servant, assigned the task of caring for God's people; but the shepherd must remember that the flock belongs to God, not to him. The New Testament writers continue to describe Jesus as the Chief Shepherd, who provides the role model for all under-shepherds (e.g. Heb. 13:20; 1 Pet. 2:25; 5:4; Rev. 7:17).

In 1 Peter 5, no specific duties for the shepherd are described; it is probably assumed that the functions of feeding, leading, nurturing, protecting, and so forth would be evident from the observation of actual shepherds, or from passages like Psalm 23 or Ezekiel 34 that develop the analogy more fully. In Ephesians 4, Paul cites another function for the human shepherd, along with several other types of leaders in the church, i.e. apostles, prophets, evangelists, and teachers, who are grouped under a single definite article with the 'pastors / shepherds', indicating that we should speak of pastor-teachers, rather than of two separate groups. These leadership gifts, says Paul, are given 'to prepare God's people for works of service' (v. 12), with the result that the whole community becomes unified and mature.

The shepherd image is one of the few that is applied exclusively to leaders, and not to members of the community as a whole. Therefore, it becomes a very important image for understanding what is distinctive about the role of leadership. Although many other images, like 'brother' or 'fellow-servant', express the equality of every member of the fellowship, a term like 'shepherd' reminds us that even on the human level, some are responsible to lead while others follow, and some have authority while others are called to respond to that authority. Christ is not the *only* shepherd; he has appointed human shepherds to assist him. The shepherd image conveys ideas of tenderness, nurture, and devotion; but it also implies discipline (the rod and the staff), the setting of limits (protection against wolves), and the right to establish direction (leading to pasture). In fact, the verb 'to shepherd' (*poimaino*) is sometimes translated as 'rule' (Rev. 2:27; 12:5; 19:15; cf. Ps. 2:9).

Soil

In Hebrews 6:7–8 the author pictures two types of land or soil (*ge*). As in Jesus' parable of the soils, the contrast is between land that produces and land that does not. Both drink in the rain that falls on them; and both are intended to be useful to those for whom they are being farmed. In the first case, the land produces a useful crop and receives the blessing of God. But in the second case, the land produces only thorns and thistles; it is worthless, in danger of being cursed (though still not abandoned as utterly worthless), and in the end is burned (a common farmer's solution for dealing with a weed-infested field, in order to prepare it for the next planting season). Similarly, the believer receives blessings from God for a purpose; he or she is expected to produce something useful for the Lord with these resources and opportunities; something of value is supposed to grow in and through his or her life.

SOLDIER

On all three occasions that Paul uses the term 'soldier' (*stratiotes*) or 'fellow-soldier' (*systratiotes*), he is writing from prison, surrounded by Roman soldiers. He refers to Epaphroditus (Phil. 2:25) and to Archippus (Philem. 2) as his fellow-soldiers. He urges Timothy in 2 Timothy 2:3,4:

> Endure hardship with us like a good soldier (*stratiotes*) of Christ Jesus. No-one serving as a soldier (*strateuomenos*) gets involved in civilian affairs – he wants to please his commanding officer (*stratologesanti*).

The image of the soldier implies a life of discipline, struggle, and hardship. It implies strict accountability to one's superior. Notice that Paul does not compare himself to the general, with his fellow-Christians as the troops. Rather, he describes the others as fellow-soldiers, all under the same commanding officer, Jesus Christ.

Other passages also refer to the image of warfare for the Christian life, though not employing the noun 'soldier'.

For example, in 2 Corinthians 10:3,4 Paul speaks of waging spiritual warfare (*stratiometha*) with divinely powerful weapons (*strateias*). In 1 Timothy 1:18 he exhorts Timothy to 'Fight (*strateuei*) the good fight (*strateian*)'. Of course, there is also the well-known passage in Ephesians 6 where Paul describes the full armour (*panoplian*) of God (v. 11) which the Christian is to wear in the struggle against the devil (cf. 1 Thess. 5:8). The apostle Peter also uses the military image in 1 Peter 2:11 where he warns against the sinful desires 'which wage war (*strateuontai*) against your soul' (cf. Jas. 4:1).

STAR (see LIGHT)

STEWARD (see MANAGER)

STONE

In 1 Peter 2, Jesus is described as 'the living Stone (*lithon*)' (v. 4), the cornerstone (v. 6), the capstone (v. 7), and a stumbling stone (v. 8). In verse 5 Peter describes believers as 'living stones' who come to Jesus to be built into a spiritual house. It seems that 'stone' is not a sufficiently dynamic image to capture the phenomenon of growth and the pulse of new life that energizes the community of believers. Hence Peter speaks of 'living' stones.

The metaphor of the building speaks not only of the believers' special relationship to God – as his dwelling place, as those who belong to him, and as those who are built upon Jesus the cornerstone and foundation – but also of their relationship to one another. They have been fitted together with the same skill employed by a stonemason, each stone carefully placed in relation to the ones around it, each one doing its part to hold up the entire structure, together fulfilling the purpose of providing a dwelling place for the Holy Spirit.

STRANGER (see RESIDENT, TEMPORARY)

T

TEACHER

A very common role described in the early Christian community is that of the 'teacher' (*didaskalos*). The leadership of the Antioch church was apparently comprised of 'prophets and teachers' (Acts 13:1). This word appears in two of the lists of spiritual gifts: in 1 Corinthians 12:28 it is cited third, grouped with the apostles and prophets; in Ephesians 4:11 it appears after apostles, prophets, and evangelists, in a sort of 'hyphenated' form with 'pastors', thus 'pastor-teachers (*tous de poimenas kai didaskalous*)'. Twice Paul says that he himself was appointed as a teacher (1 Tim. 2:7; 2 Tim. 1:11). James 3:1 warns that 'not many of you should presume to be teachers' because teachers will be evaluated more stringently by the Lord.

Each of the references cited so far views the role of teacher as a function performed not by everyone in the church, but only by those who are gifted and appointed to do so. However, the author of Hebrews points to a broader application of the teaching role. In 5:12 he scolds his readers for their immaturity, saying, 'though by this time you ought to be teachers, you need someone to teach you the elementary truths of God's word all over again'. In this context every believer is expected to become a teacher, able to communicate the basic truths of the Christian message to others. Thus the ability to teach is an index of maturity.

In the gospels, where Jesus is often called 'teacher', the emphasis is not on mere acquisition of knowledge but on prompt application of the truth that has been heard (e.g. Mt. 7:24–27; Mk. 3:35; Mt. 28:20). So then, the teacher in the early church could never be content with accumulation of facts unaccompanied by changes in attitude and behaviour.

Another word used for teaching in the Christian community is *katecheo*, which means to pass on information about something. Luke opens his gospel by explaining that he wants Theophilus to 'know the certainty of the things you have been taught (*katechethes*)' (1:4). In Acts 18:25, Luke describes Apollos as one who 'had been instructed in the way of the Lord'. In Romans 2:18 Paul rebukes the pride of the person who brags that he has been 'instructed by the law'. Galatians 6:6 contains directions about how the community should provide for its teachers: 'Anyone who receives instruction (*katechoumenos*) in the word must share all good things with his instructor (*katechounti*).'

TEMPLE

Although several words related to 'building' are used by the New Testament writers to describe Christians, the word 'temple' (*naos*), which is derived from *naio* (to dwell), is used in contexts which focus on the indwelling presence of the Spirit of God. *Naos* refers more specifically to the sanctuary, whereas the other word translated 'temple' (*hieron*) denotes the whole complex of temple buildings in Jerusalem.

The temple metaphor is used by Paul, especially in the Corinthian correspondence. In 1 Corinthians 3, Paul is teaching about the need for unity, rebuking the divisive spirits of those who want to rally around different leaders. He speaks of the Corinthians as 'God's building' (v. 9), then describes the differences in role between the one who lays the foundation and the others that build upon it. Next he asks:

> Don't you know that you yourselves are God's temple (*naos*) and that God's Spirit lives in you? If anyone destroys God's temple, God will destroy him; for God's temple is sacred, and you are that temple (3:16,17).

The community as a whole is of immense value to God. It is set apart as the place where his Holy Spirit dwells. Therefore, to do anything to disrupt the unity and peace of that sanctuary is to incur the judgement of God. The place where God has chosen to live must be treated with respect.

A few chapters later, Paul warns against sexual immorality, saying:

> Do you not know that your body is a temple (*naos*) of the Holy Spirit, who is in you, whom you have received from God? You are not your own; you were bought at a price. Therefore honour God with your body (6:19,20).

The repetition of the accusing question 'Do you not know?' implies that these are elementary teachings of which even the newest Christian should be aware. Again, the focus of the temple image is that God lives there. The great value that God ascribes to his people is implied in the price that was paid for their redemption. This image also points to the believer's accountability to God; the body is *God's* temple; it must be used only in ways appropriate to the presence of a holy God.

In 2 Corinthians 6 Paul introduces the image of the temple once again, this time as the basis for a warning not to be 'yoked with unbelievers', but rather to live lives of separation from the world. He asks: 'What agreement is there between the temple of God and idols? For we are the temple of the living God' (6:16). Then he alludes to some Old Testament passages (Lev. 26:12; Ezek. 37:27) which speak of God living and walking among his people. Thus, once again, the image of the temple is associated with the presence of God, and hence with the need for complete holiness.

Another reference to the temple of God occurs in Ephesians 2. There Paul describes the church as a building founded on the apostles and prophets, with Jesus Christ as the cornerstone, which 'rises to become a holy temple in the Lord' (v. 21), a 'dwelling in which God lives by his Spirit' (v. 22). Again, the presence of God is the key distinctive of the temple. It is the indwelling and purifying presence of God which gives dignity to the life of the individual believer and which makes the community of believers worthy of respect, no matter how much the world may demean them, reject them, or persecute them.

TWELVE

All four gospel writers refer to the disciples on a number of occasions as 'the twelve' (e.g. Mt. 26:14; Mk. 4:10; Lk.

18:31; Jn. 20:24). But only once is it recorded that Jesus himself referred to them by this term. In John 6:70, when many were turning back and no longer following him, Jesus said, 'Have I not chosen you, the Twelve (*dodeka*)? Yet one of you is a devil!'

The emphasis on Jesus' choice of these twelve, and the correspondence to the twelve tribes of God's chosen people Israel, suggest that a deeper symbolic significance is implied in the number. Jesus did not just happen to choose twelve, rather than eight, or fifteen. In Matthew 19:28, on the road to Jerusalem, and again during the Last Supper, in Luke 22:30, Jesus promises his disciples that in the coming kingdom they will sit on twelve thrones, judging the twelve tribes of Israel. This promise suggests that the disciples represent the new Israel, the new people of God drawn together by their allegiance to the Messiah. But it also implies that they will have leadership roles in the believing community, both in this age and in the age to come.

Twice outside the gospels the group of apostles are called 'the Twelve'. In Acts 6:2, we read that 'the Twelve gathered all the disciples together' to resolve the problem of equitable food distribution among the widows. Then, in 1 Corinthians 15:5, Paul says that Jesus appeared to Peter 'and then to the Twelve'. Thus even Paul recognizes the special identity of this original group of apostles.

In the book of Acts we see the twelve forming a leadership team in the Jerusalem fellowship, not only taking the primary role in teaching the Word and in prayer, but also providing overall direction to the community. Yet the twelve do not remain long as an identifiable leadership group. In Acts 15 the decisions are made by the 'apostles and elders' (vv. 2,4,6,22,23), and by Acts 21 only the elders are mentioned (v. 18) with James, not the apostle but rather the brother of Jesus, as the most visible leader. Thus after the initial phase of establishing the church, the twelve begin to recede into the background; there is no attempt to perpetuate the group as such after the martyrdom of James the apostle in Acts 12:2. This term, then, as important as it is in the founding of the church, is not one which can be applied to any group of believers or church leaders living today.

V

VESSEL

An image that portrays the Christian life as one of service is 'vessel' (*skeuos*), also translated as 'instrument' and 'jar'. In Acts 9:15 the Lord tells Ananias that Paul is 'my chosen instrument (*skeuos*) to carry my name before the Gentiles and their kings and before the people of Israel'. Paul says to the Corinthians that 'we have this treasure in jars (*skeuesin*) of clay to show that this all-surpassing power is from God and not from us' (2 Cor. 4:7). The 'treasure' is the life of Jesus in us (v. 10); the containers are our weak, fallible bodies and human natures. Paul contrasts household articles used for noble purposes with those used for ignoble purposes, and urges Timothy to be an 'instrument (*skeuos*) for noble purposes, made holy, useful to the Master and prepared to do any good work' (2 Tim. 2:21). In each case, the emphasis of this image of the vessel is on the task. The Christian has a job to do; it may be 'any good work', or more specifically the task of proclaiming the gospel. Although the image of the vessel is applied specifically to Christian leaders in two of the passages, it is equally appropriate for any believer.

W

WITNESS

The word 'witness' (*martys*) originally comes from the legal arena, and means one who gives evidence in a trial, both in classical Greek and in Old Testament usage. The role of the witness was to attest to the reality of certain events in a public setting. Thus the witness had a twofold role – to verify the evidence, that is, to heighten the credibility of the statements made; and secondly, to proclaim the truth to others, making the facts known publicly. The witness was someone who had had an experience, who could testify to what he had seen or heard personally (cf. 1 Jn. 1:1–13).

After explaining to the disciples how all the events of his suffering, death, and resurrection were fulfilments of Scripture, Jesus said to them: 'You are witnesses (*martyres*) of these things' (Lk. 24:48). Similarly, in Acts 1:8, Jesus' final words to his disciples are recorded by the author Luke: 'You will be my witnesses in Jerusalem, and in all Judea and Samaria, and to the ends of the earth'. Here the emphasis shifts from witness to *events* to witness on behalf of a *person*. In both passages there is an emphasis on the nations – Luke 24:47 says that 'repentance and forgiveness of sins will be preached in his name to all nations, beginning at Jerusalem'.

Other variations of the same metaphor occur several times in Jesus' conversations with his disciples. In sending out the twelve, Jesus says, 'On my account you will be brought before governors and kings as witnesses to them and to the Gentiles' (Mt. 10:18). The witness is the one who gives the word of testimony, while the 'testimony' (*martyrion*) refers to the word given. Notice again the reference to the nations. In his account of the Olivet discourse, Mark includes the same phrase, 'as witnesses to them', and follows it with another explicit reference to the nations: 'And the gospel must first be preached to all nations' (Mk. 13:10; cf. Lk. 21:13, where there is reference to the testimony, but not to the nations).

One more example is found in John 15:27, where Jesus uses the related verb after warning the disciples of the persecutions they will suffer because of their identification with him: 'You also must testify (*martyreite*), for you have been with me from the beginning'.

In summary, then, the image of the 'witness' is associated by Jesus with first-hand experience, public proclamation, worldwide ministry, and the suffering of persecution.

The book of Acts gives many illustrations of the continued usage of this term. Matthias is appointed to replace Judas because, as Peter says, 'one of these must become a witness with us of his resurrection' (1:22). Again and again in his preaching Peter continues to insist that he and others are witnesses of the resurrection (2:32; 3:15; 5:32; 10:39,41). According to Paul, both Ananias and the risen Jesus had told Paul that he was being appointed as a witness (22:15; 26:16). Two other individuals are called witnesses:

Paul refers to Stephen as the Lord's witness (Acts 22:20); and Jesus, addressing the church at Pergamum in John's vision, alludes to 'Antipas, my faithful witness' (Rev. 2:13). In each of the latter two cases, the idea of witness is associated with someone who remained faithful to the point of death for Christ's sake. But the basic idea of the word 'witness' is not someone who lays down his life, but rather someone who reports what he has personally seen and heard. In each of the references in the book of Acts, those described as 'witnesses' are those who actually saw the risen Christ – including Stephen, who saw the heavens opened and Jesus as the Son of Man standing at the right hand of God (7:56), as well as Paul, who met Jesus on the road to Damascus (9:3–6).

The same emphasis on personal observation is maintained in the other New Testament uses of the word. Paul alludes to the confession that Timothy made 'in the presence of many witnesses' (1 Tim. 6:12) and later urges him to pass on what he heard from Paul 'in the presence of many witnesses' (2 Tim. 2:2). In his first letter Peter makes his appeal to the elders as a fellow elder and as 'a witness of Christ's sufferings' (1 Pet. 5:1).

In the New Testament, when the image of the witness is used to describe followers of Jesus, it always refers to people who have personally experienced Jesus. Thus the metaphor strongly emphasizes the aspect of personal identification; it does not allow for second-hand reporting.

WORKER

In Matthew 9:37,38, when he saw the helplessness and spiritual needs of the crowds who constantly pursued him,

Jesus addressed his disciples: 'The harvest is plentiful but the workers (*ergatai*) are few. Ask the Lord of the harvest, therefore, to send out workers (*ergatas*) into his harvest field.'

The metaphor 'worker' stresses the task, as well as the link of accountability between the workers and the Lord of the harvest. As we see in Matthew 10, the disciples became the answer to their own prayer. They themselves became the workers thrust out into the field. They did not volunteer, but were sent out. The word translated 'send out' (*ekbale*) may imply a forceful act, in view of the possible reluctance of the one sent.

In Luke 10:2, when Jesus sends out the 72, the same call to prayer for workers is issued. Both Matthew 10 and Luke 10 record Jesus' saying, 'The labourer (*ergates*) is worthy of his hire', as justification for the disciples to receive food and lodging from those to whom they preach.

Jesus refers to the work of the disciples as a kind of harvesting in John 4 as well. After speaking with the woman by the well in Samaria, he prepares the disciples for the great spiritual response which they are about to encounter among the townspeople, saying, 'Open your eyes and look at the fields! They are ripe for harvest . . . I sent you to reap what you have not worked for' (4:35,38).

In Matthew 20 the term 'worker' appears once again when Jesus tells the parable of the workers in the vineyard. The owner of the vineyard is called 'landowner' (*oikodespotes*) in verses 1 and 11, and 'the owner of the vineyard' (*ho kurios tou ampelonos*) in verse 8. Both terms emphasize that he is the one in authority. The owner goes out to hire workers (*ergatas*). Different ones are enlisted to work at various hours of the day, but all receive the same wages at the end. The parable as a whole teaches that the Lord has the sole right to determine how his servants are rewarded. Any complaints are evidence of ingratitude and lack of submission. Thus the image of 'worker' is associated with a task to be done, with submission and accountability to the Lord's authority, and with the prospect of ultimate reward.

The image of the disciple as 'worker' (*ergates*) or 'fellow-worker' (*synergos*) is also a favourite of Paul's. In 2 Timothy 2:15 he urges Timothy to present himself approved to God as a 'workman (*ergaten*) who does not need to be ashamed and who correctly handles the word of truth'. The verb translated 'correctly handle' (*orthotomeo*), used in the Greek translation of Proverbs 3:6 and 11:5, means to cut a straight path; it conveys the image of a road builder cutting through a thick forest, or a traveller trying to make his way through thick underbrush.

In his letters Paul makes frequent reference to those who have collaborated in ministry with him as his 'fellow-workers'. He applies the term 'fellow-worker' (*synergos*) to Priscilla and Aquila (Rom. 16:3), Urbanus (Rom. 16:9), Timothy (Rom. 16:21; 1 Thess. 3:2), Titus (2 Cor. 8:23), Epaphroditus (Phil. 2:25), Clement (Phil. 4:3), Mark (Col. 4:11; Philem. 24), Jesus called Justus (Col. 4:11), Philemon (Philem. 1), Aristarchus, Demas, and Luke (Philem. 24).

The term 'fellow-worker' implies a dimension of equality. The emphasis is not on one person being over while the other is under; rather, both are labouring toward a common goal. Thus in addressing the Corinthian spirit of favouritism for one leader over another, Paul says of himself and Apollos, 'We are God's fellow-workers' (1 Cor. 3:9). In his second letter to the Corinthians, Paul speaks sadly of the disciplinary function he had to perform on a previous visit, softening his tone by saying, 'Not that we lord it over

your faith, but we work with you (*synergoi*) for your joy'
(1:24). Before God, who commissioned the task, all the
workers stand on the same level.

Yet there can still be a dimension of authority in the
expression 'God's fellow-worker'. When the focus is on
being fellow-workers with other Christians, the emphasis
is on equality. But when the focus is on working together
with God, then the ones who speak on behalf of God
convey God's authority in their words. Thus Paul exhorts
the Corinthians later in his second letter: 'As God's fellow
workers we urge you not to receive God's grace in vain'
(6:1).

WORKMANSHIP

In Ephesians 2:10, Paul says: 'For we are God's workman-
ship (*poiema*), created in Christ Jesus to do good works,
which God prepared in advance for us to do.' The purpose
of God's creative artistry is that we might do the good
works that have been assigned to us.

WRESTLER

In Ephesians 6:12, Paul says, 'Our struggle (*pale*) is not
against flesh and blood'. The word *pale* refers to a wrestling
match. As Paul further develops the image of struggle in
that chapter, he transforms it into the soldier involved in
hand-to-hand combat, who needs to put on the full armour
in order to withstand his adversary.

Fly on the Fence
Have you Looked at it from this Angle Before?
John Woods

'What is truth?' asked Pilate.

'Ask us' answer many Evangelicals. 'We are the people of truth. End of story.'

John Woods challenges such one-dimensional thinking. While there are tenets of our faith that *are* non-negotiable, evangelical Christians need to be aware that others may have much to teach us. Before we dismiss those who disagree with us we should ask ourselves if we have considered all God has to say on a subject.

Fly on the Fence invites us to put our preconceptions aside and take a fresh look at issues such as the Christian Sunday, worldliness, revival and Charismatics from an angle we may not have considered before.

". . . a most readable, stimulating, thought-provoking and challenging book . . . Here is a pastor's concern to give sufficient weight to the 'whole counsel of God' and not to be held captive by party lines, pet themes and hobby horses."
Malcolm Laver, General Secretary of the Fellowship of Independent Evangelical Churches.

". . . challenging, necessarily provocative and at times a little uncomfortable . . . It sends us all back to Scripture and hopefully to get closer to our brothers and sisters within the different 'evangelical tribes'.
David Abernethie

John Woods is Pastor of Lancing Tabernacle in West Sussex. He is a council member of the Fellowship of Independent Evangelical Churches.

1-85078-306-3

OM
publishing

All Churches Great and Small

A Survey of the Church Scene in the United Kingdom
C. Peter Collinson

The rich diversity in practice, organization and beliefs within Christian denominations in the UK is evidence of the vitality of British churches. But this diversity can also be bewildering for many people – especially when choosing a church.

This useful handbook of Christian churches and denominations in the UK, helps to explain what the differences are, how they have come to be and what they mean.

"A super resource book for Christian leaders. The author demonstrates a remarkable talent for simplifying complex issues without distorting them."
C. Lynn Green, Youth with a Mission.

"Peter Collinson has done the church of Jesus Christ a great service with this spiritually sensitive and well-researched book . . . His sympathetic and theologically astute treatment leaves one with an impression of the rich diversity of the British church scene rather than its fragmentation."
Derek Allan, Head of the Department for Research and Training in Mission, Baptist Union of Great Britain.

"An A–W of British churches which all students of the contemporary church scene will find invaluable . . . Just enough information about the churches without overwhelming the reader with too much detail."
Graham Horsley, Church Planting Co-ordinator, The Methodist Church.

C. Peter Collinson has served as Pastor of Baptist churches in various parts of the country, and also as a Bible College lecturer. Now retired, he lives in Carnforth, Lancashire.

1-85078-311-x

OM
publishing